Drawn by Gloria Lenzen & colored by Sabine van Ee

Drawn & colored by Lilan Chen

Global Doodle Gems Volume 12
"The Ultimate international Coloring Book...an Epic Collection from Artists around the World!"

Drawn & colored by Linda Fauconnier Tricoire

Drawn & colored by Ellen Wolters

Drawn & colored by Alexandra Rodriguez

Drawn & colored by Rover Hsiao

Drawn & colored by T.J.

Drawn & colored by Leaf Yeh

Drawn & colored by Debbie Lai

Drawn & colored by Jodi Ho

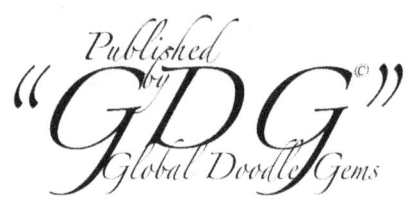

Share your colored versions with us ! We love seeing your results and hearing from you we are social !

The Official FB book page, stay on top of what we have in the works !
www.facebook.com/globaldoodlegems

The Community group, share your colored pages, meet the artists, enjoy exclusive freebies, take part in community Charity books and so much more......
www.facebook.com/groups/globaldoodlegems/

Follow us on Twitter.... @GlobalDoodlegem

We are on Instagram too
@globaldoodlegems for instagram

...and if you are not social like that we have a blog
globaldoodlegems.wordpress.com

Copyright © 2016 Global Doodle Gems

All rights are reserved by Global Doodle Gems.

Duplication of pages for personal use are allowed. You are invited to color the pages then scan/post your coloured versions to social networks, mentioning the book title and author/artist (Global Doodle Gems).

All artwork and images are protected by copyright laws. This book or any portion thereof may not, otherwise, be reproduced and/or distributed or transmitted without the express written permission of the artist/publisher of Global Doodle Gems.

All of us from the Global Doodle Gems wish you a colortastic time and look forward to seeing your wonderful color results online !

Chapter 1
Leaf Yeh

Chapter 2
Ellen Wolters

Chapter 3
Linda Fauconnier Tricoire

Chapter 4
T.J.

Chapter 5
Alexandra Rodriguez

Chapter 6
Gloria Lenzen

Chapter 7
Rover Hsiao

Chapter 8
Debbie Lai

Chapter 9
Lilan Chen

Chapter 10
Jodi Ho

Chapter 1
Leaf Yeh

Taiwan
Facebook : leaf.Painting

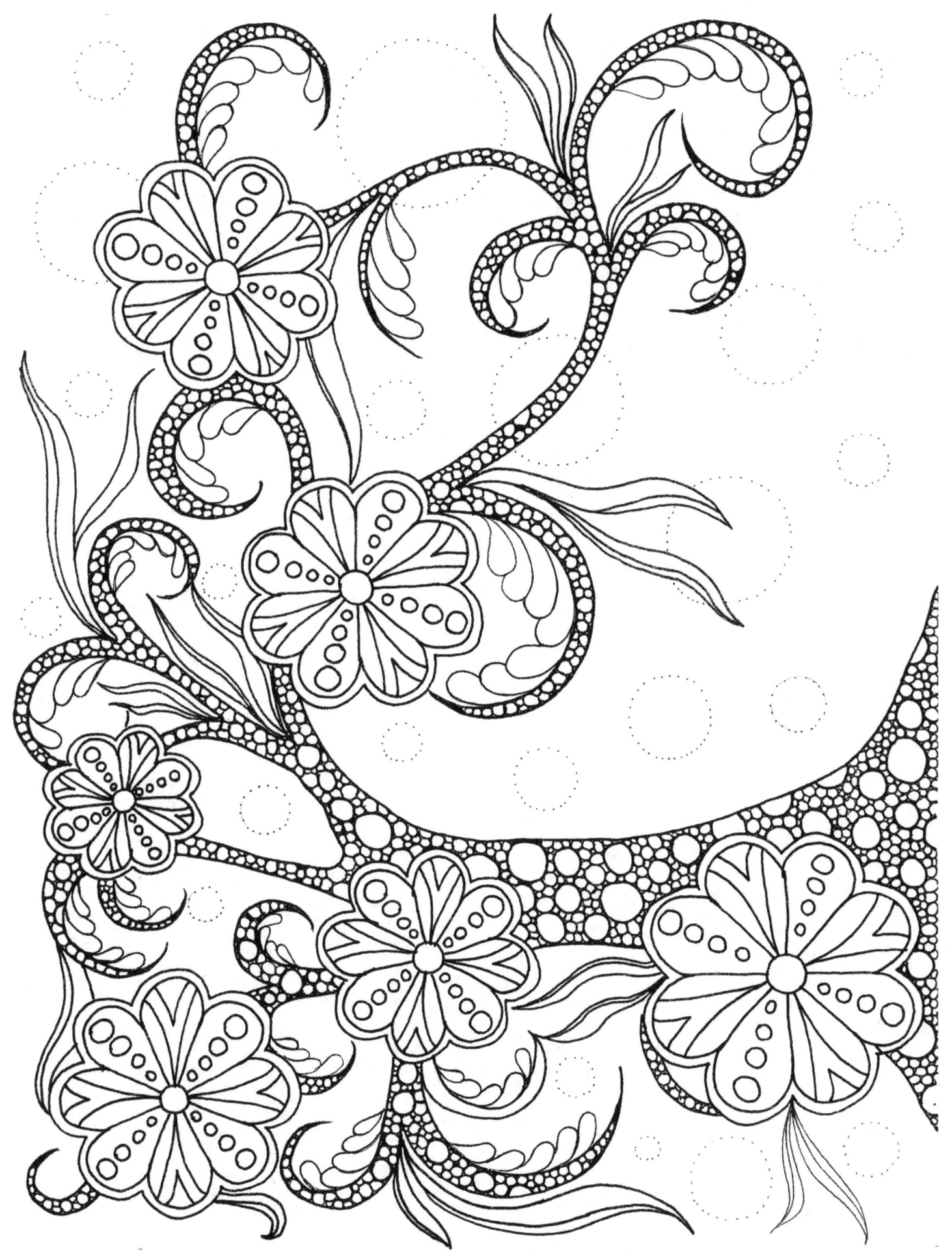

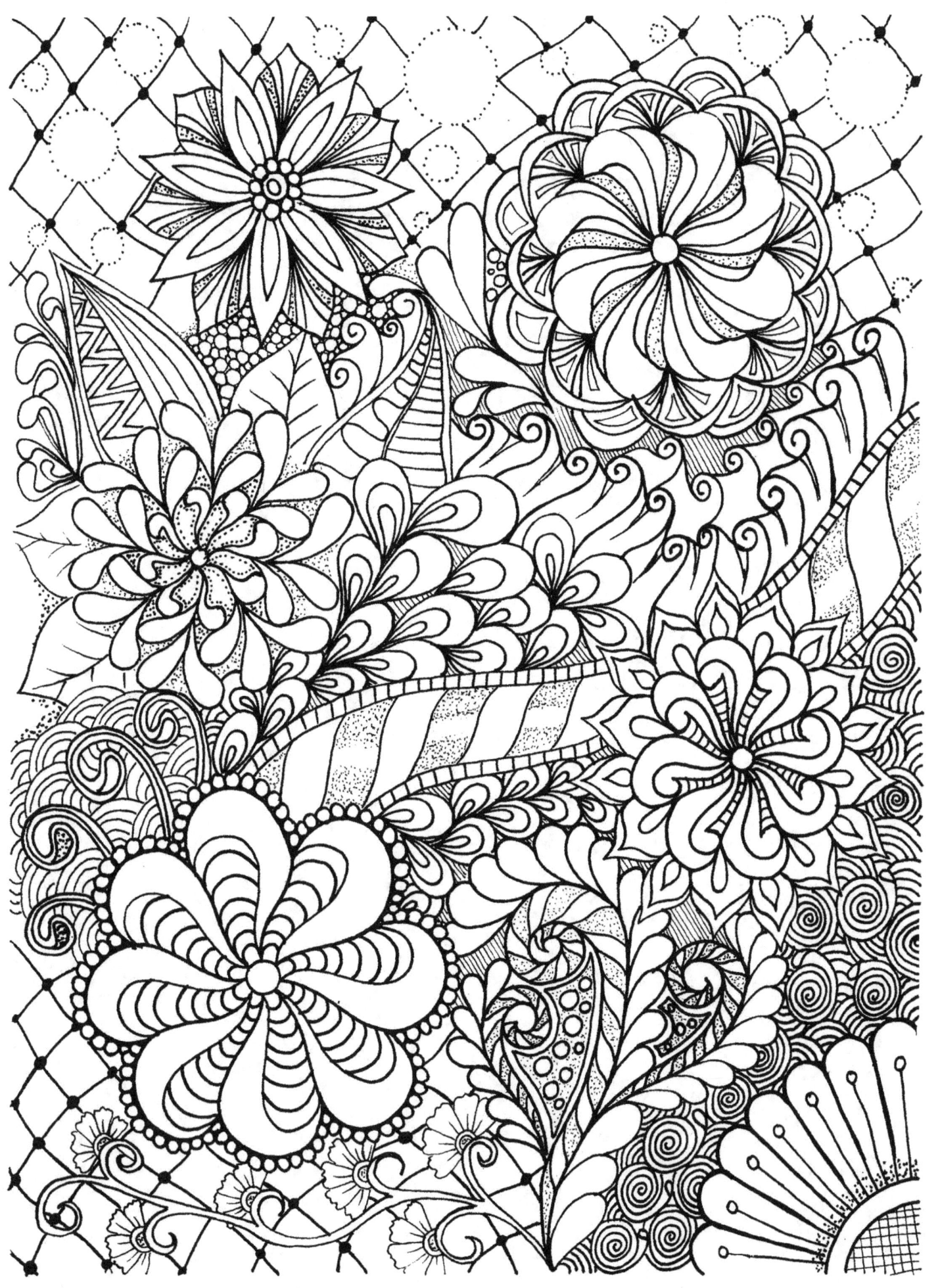

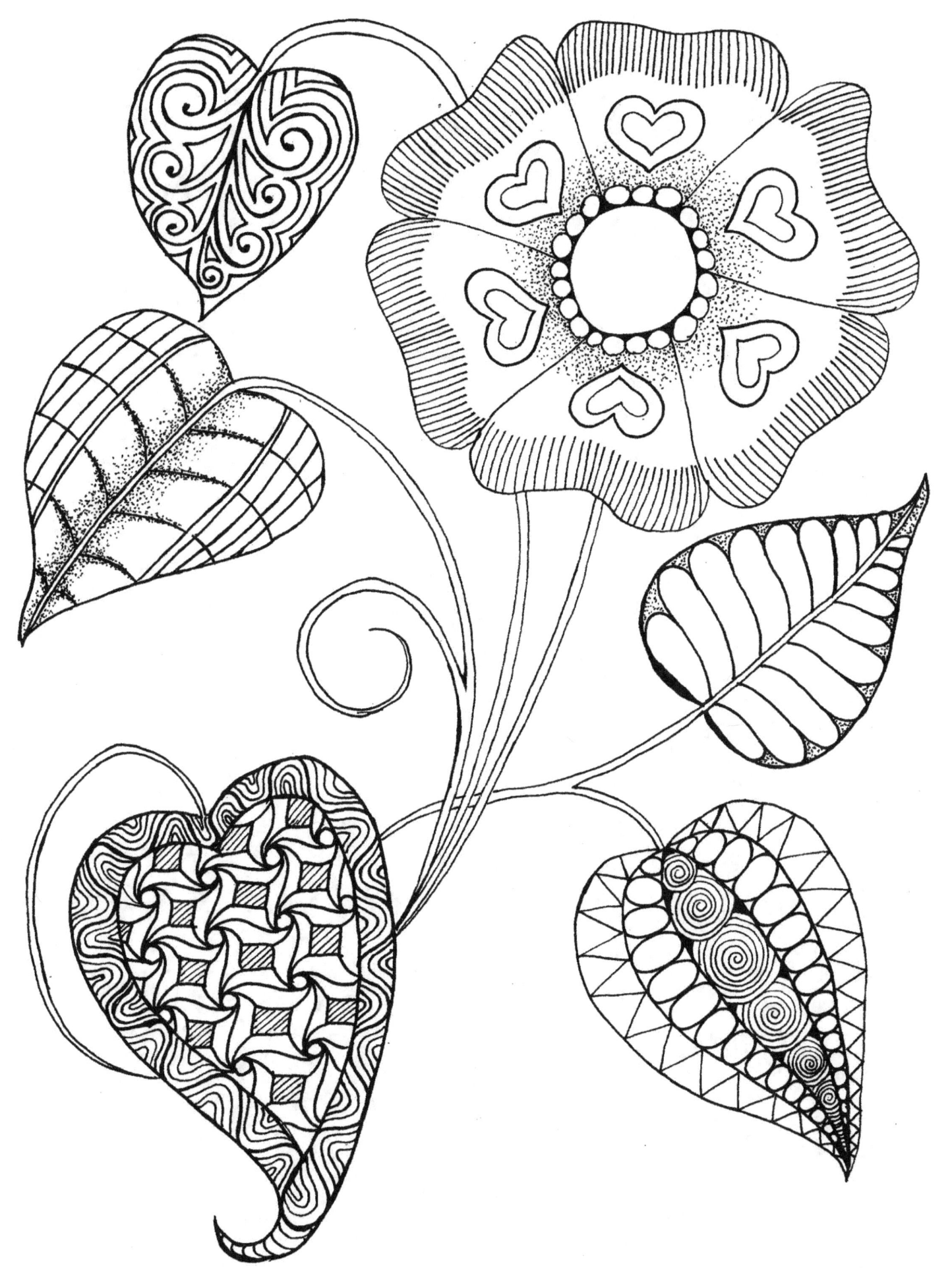

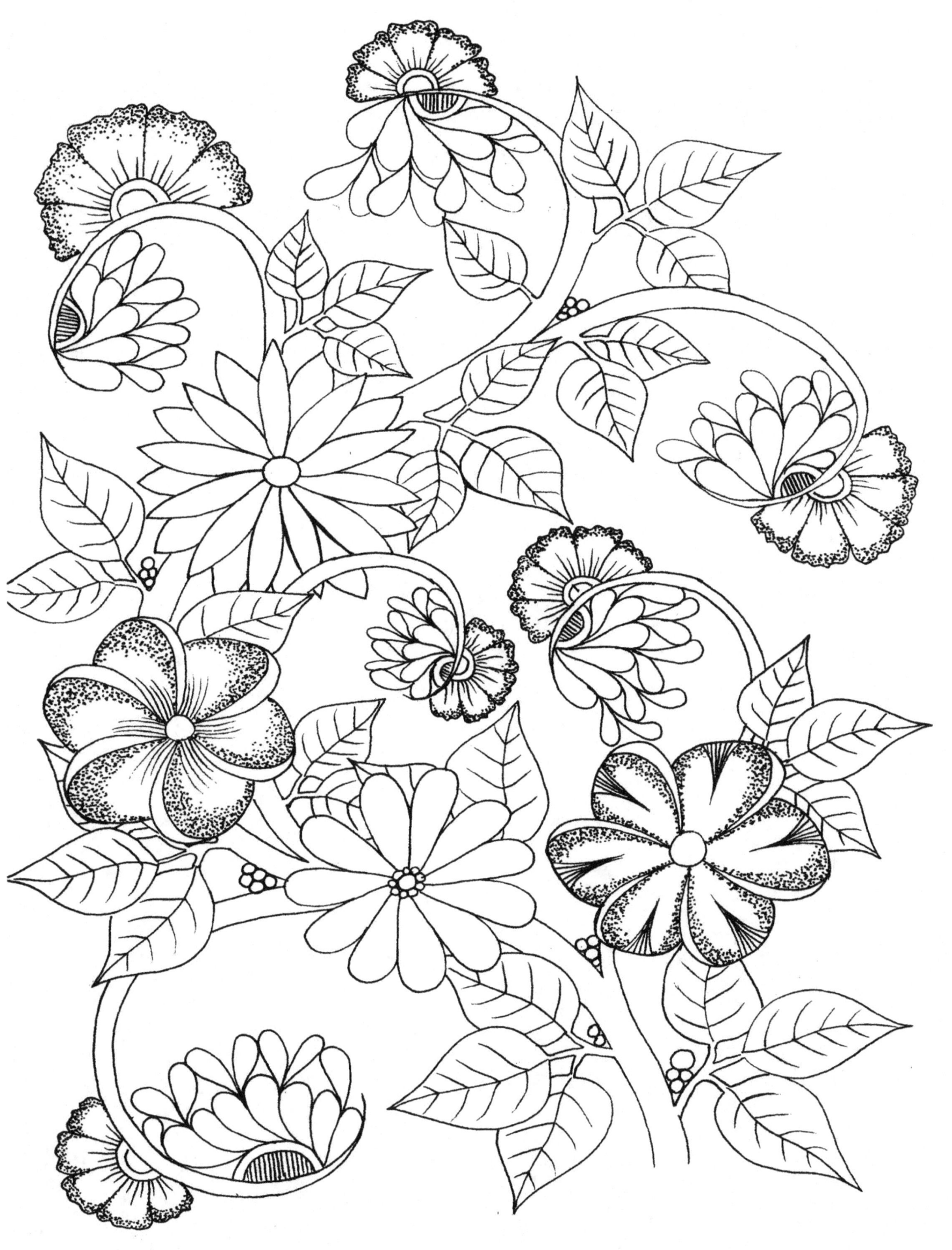

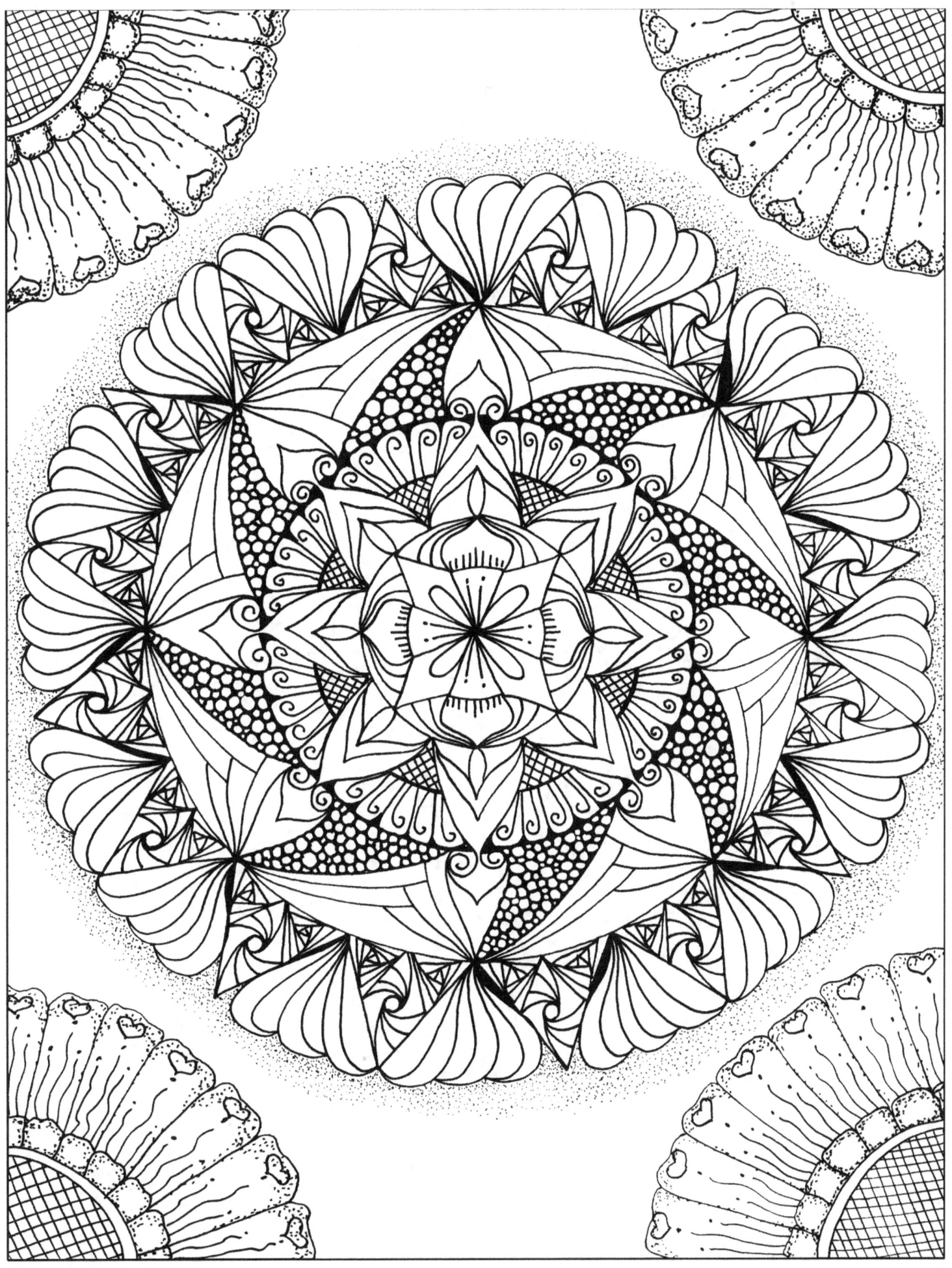

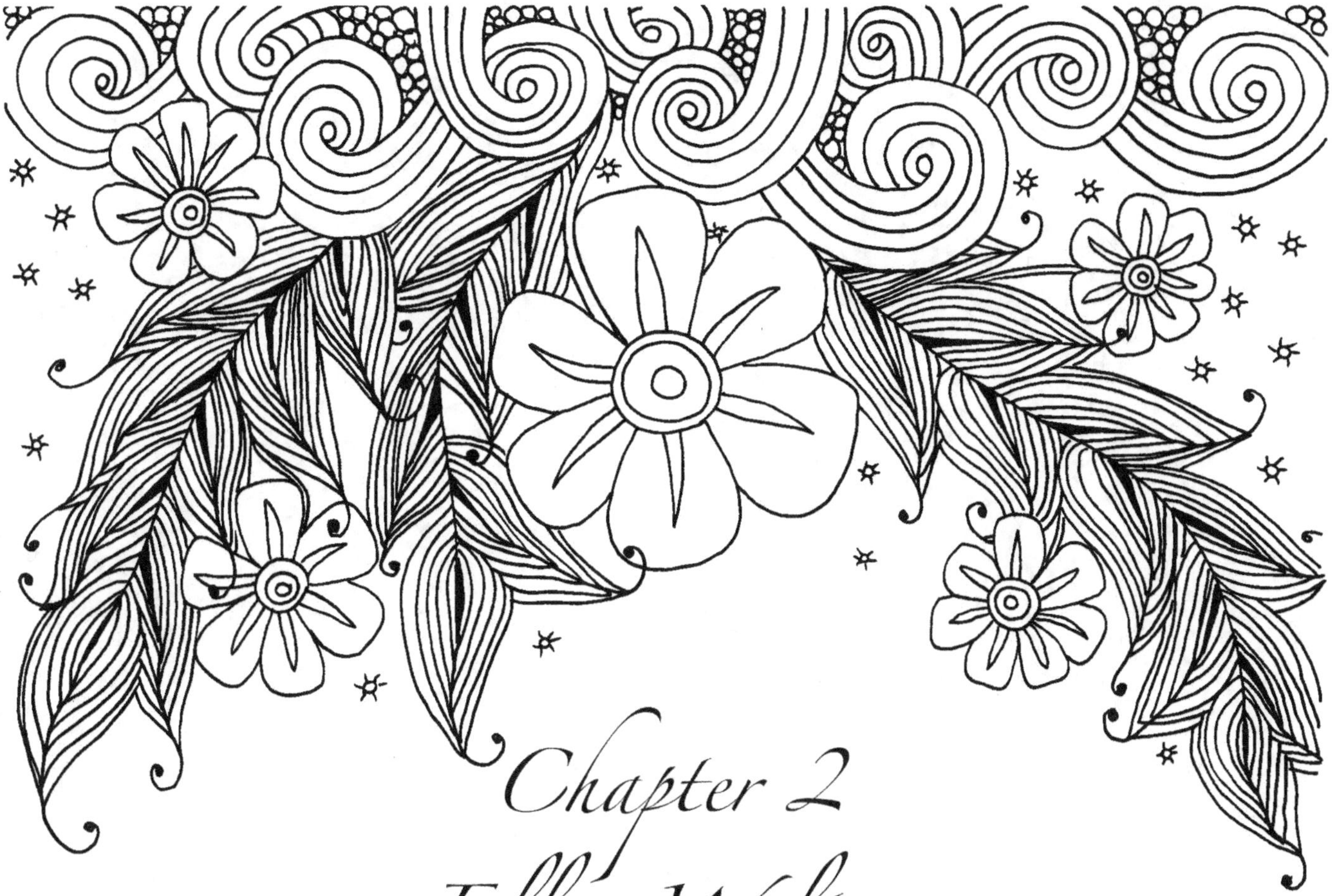

Chapter 2
Ellen Wolters

The Netherlands
http://www.tekenpraktijkdeinnerlijkewereld.blogspot.nl/
http://ellenstraties.blogspot.nl/
https://www.youtube.com/user/DIWEllenWolters

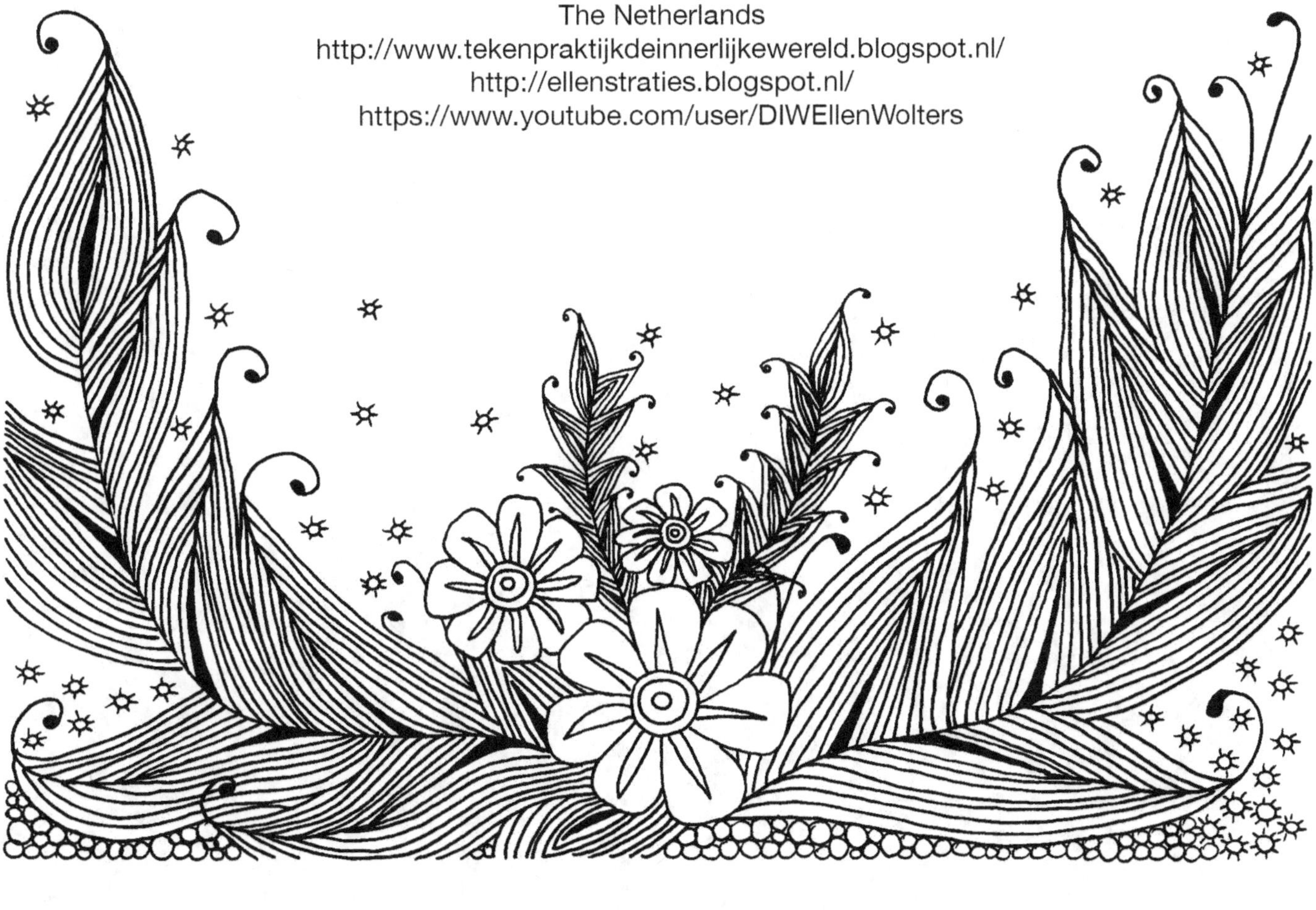

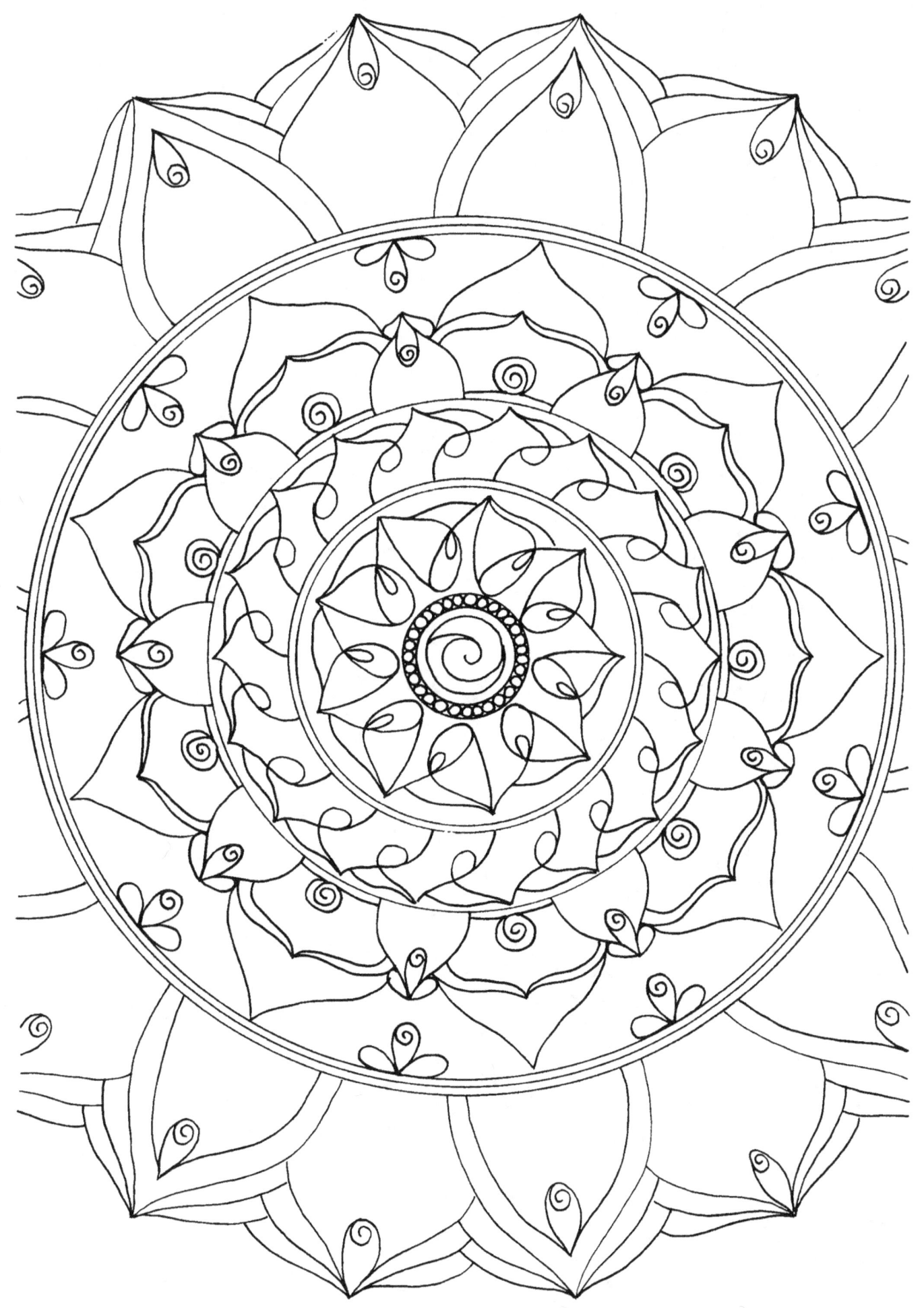

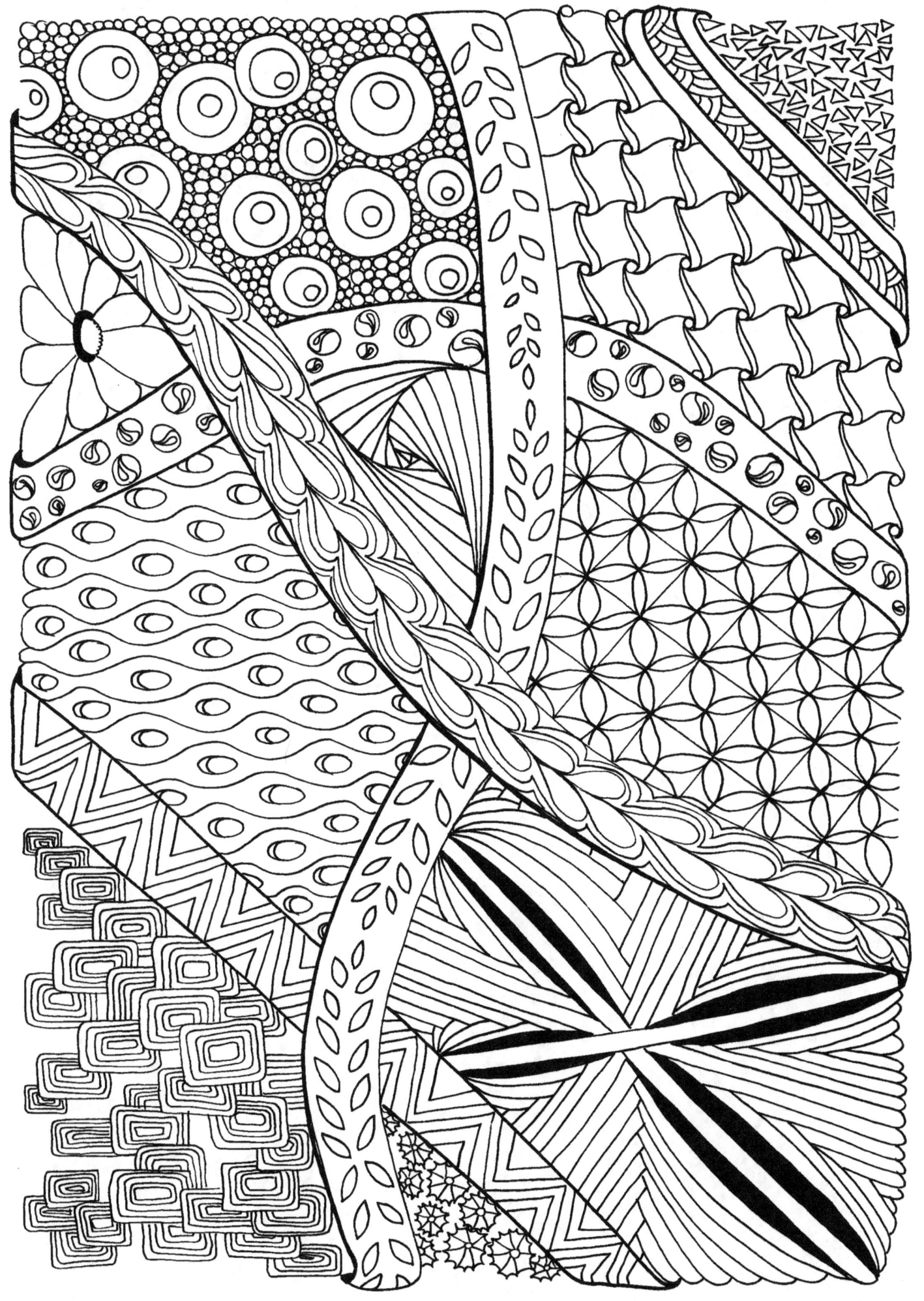

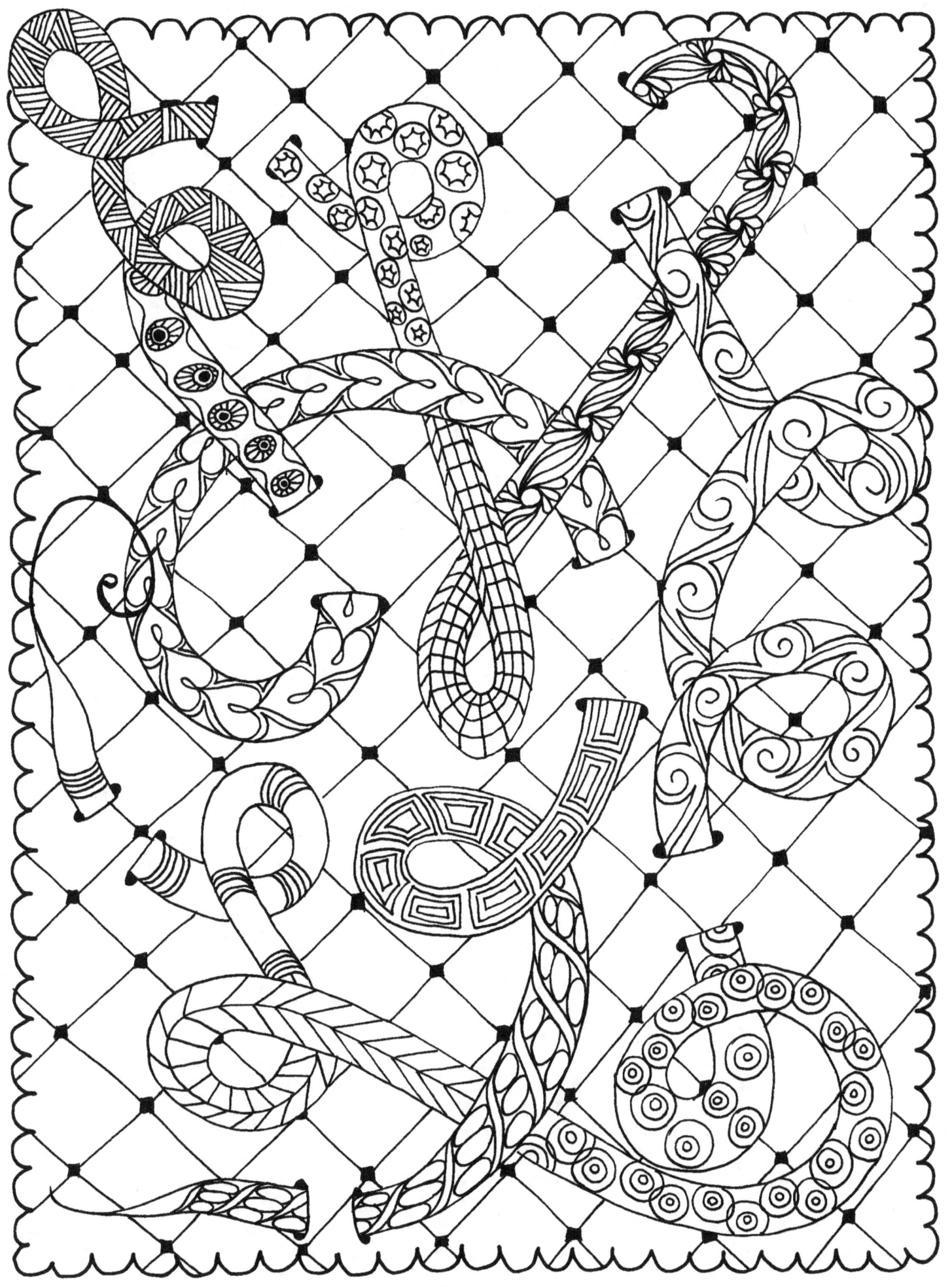

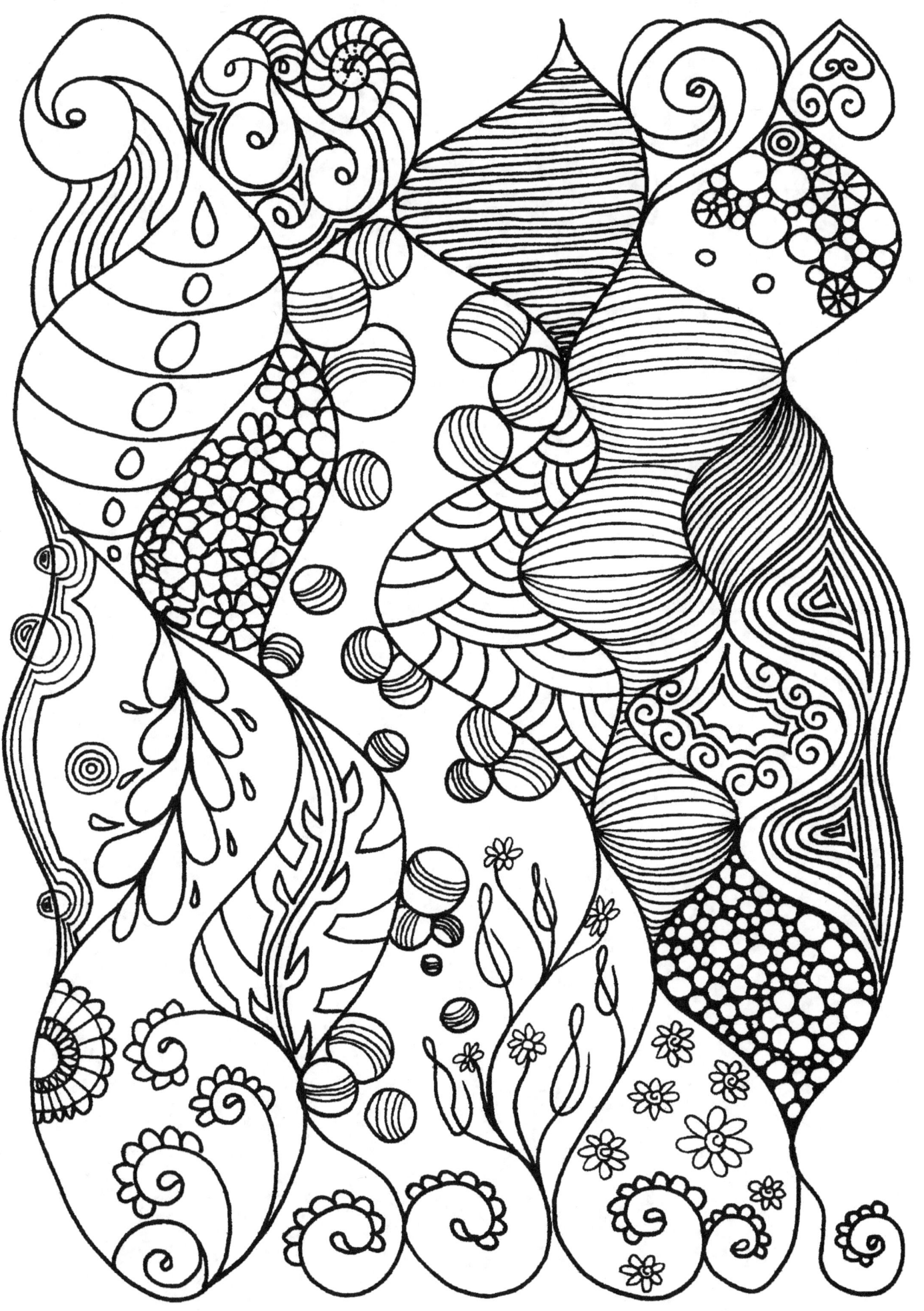

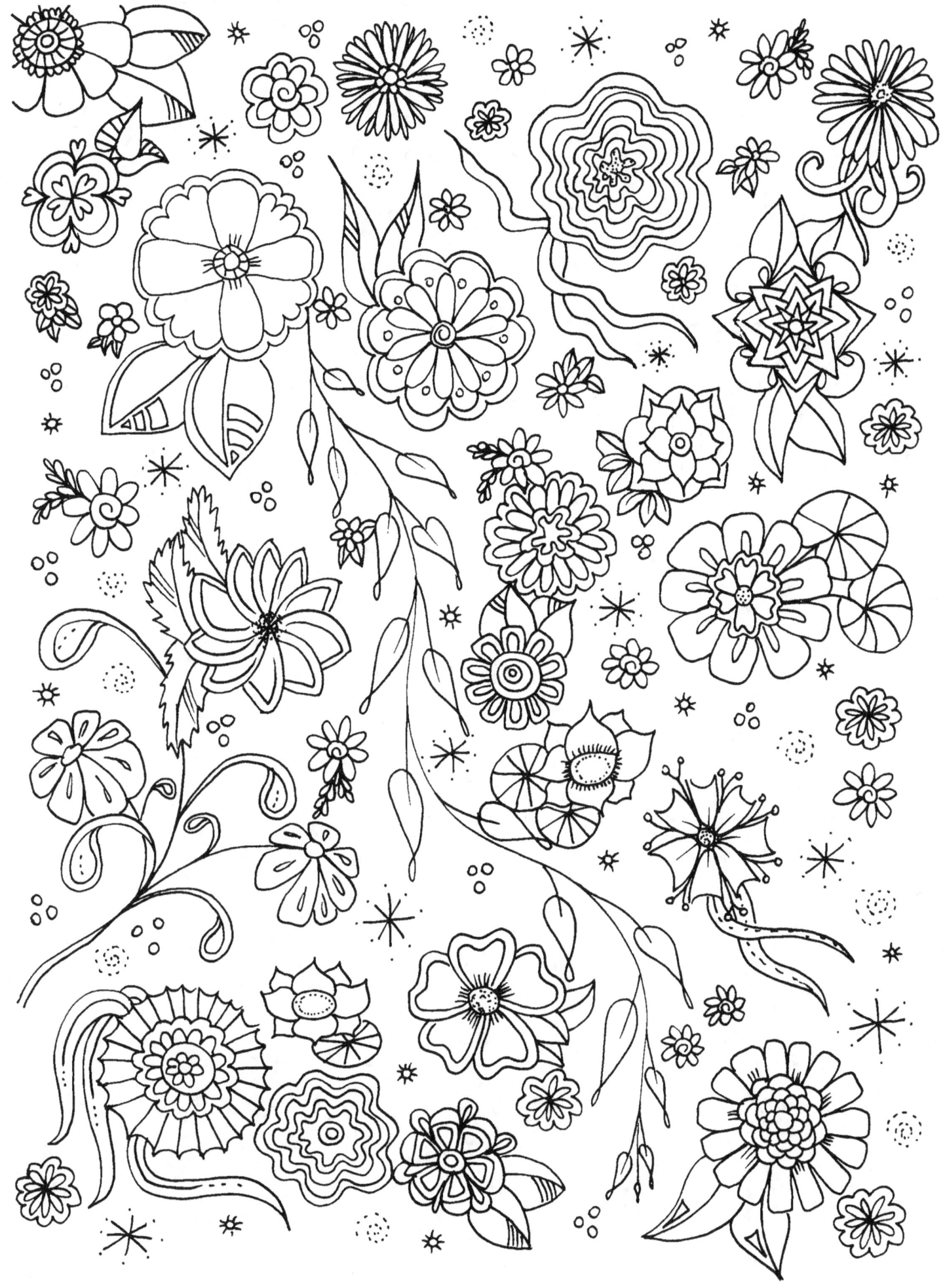

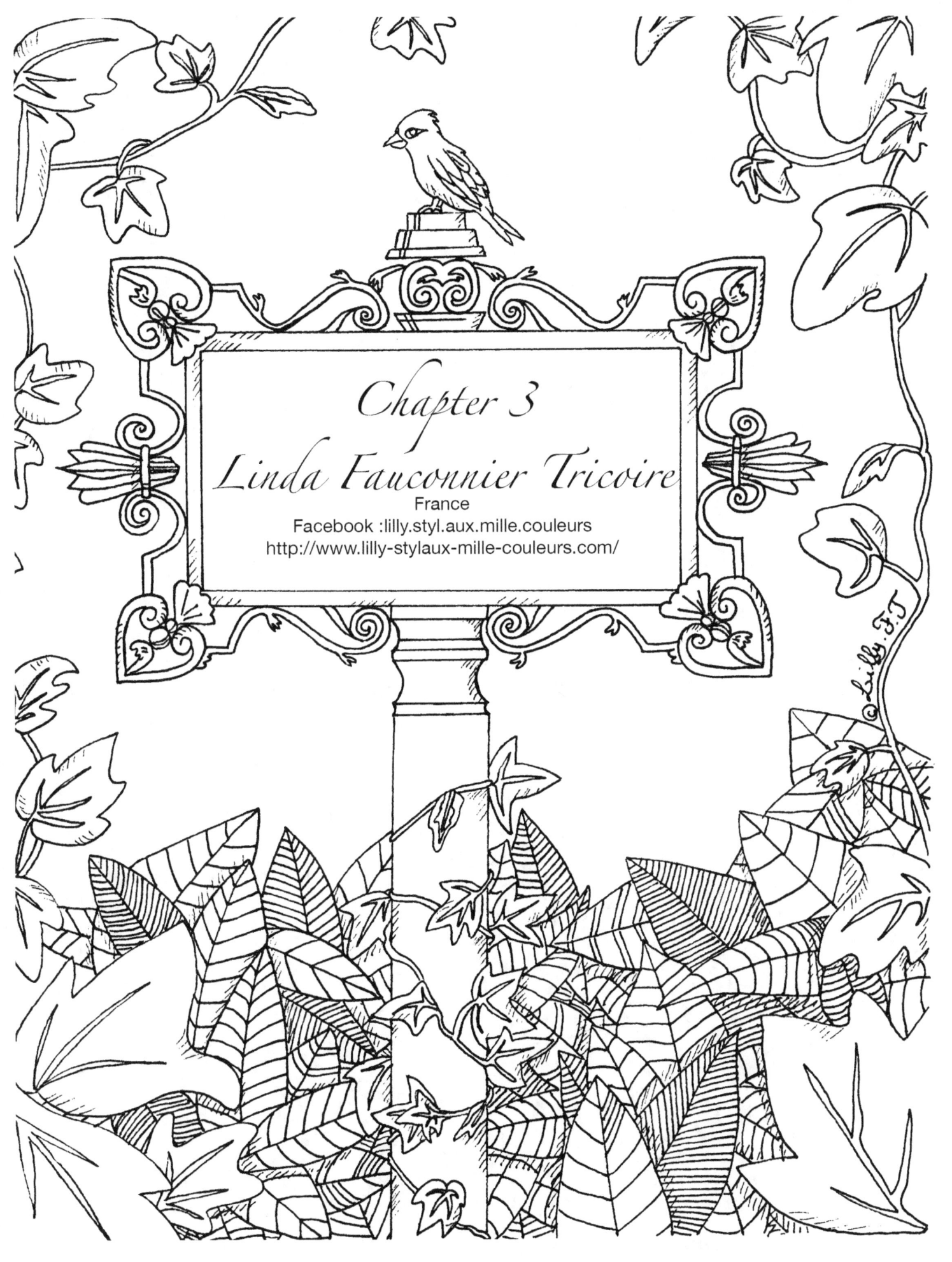

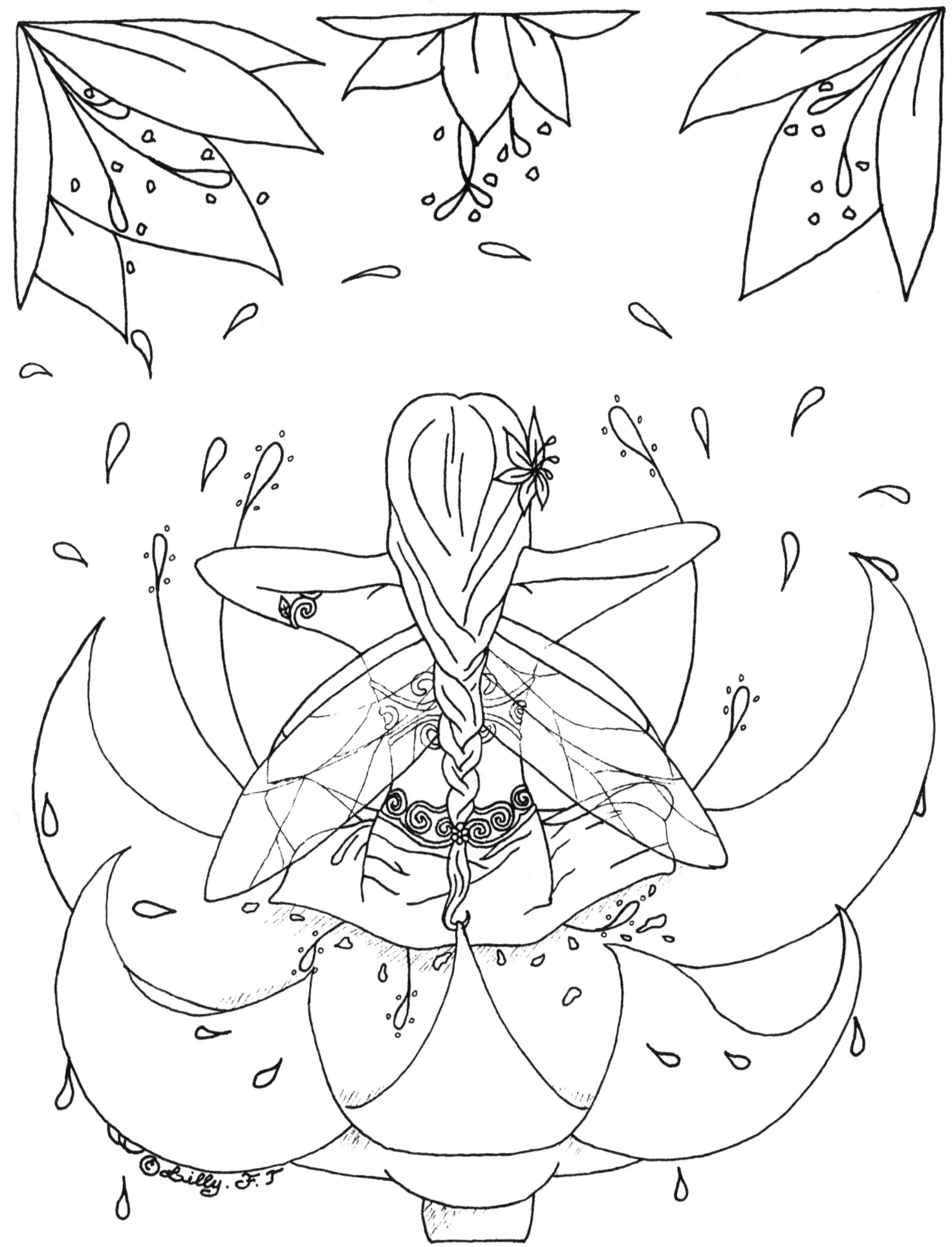

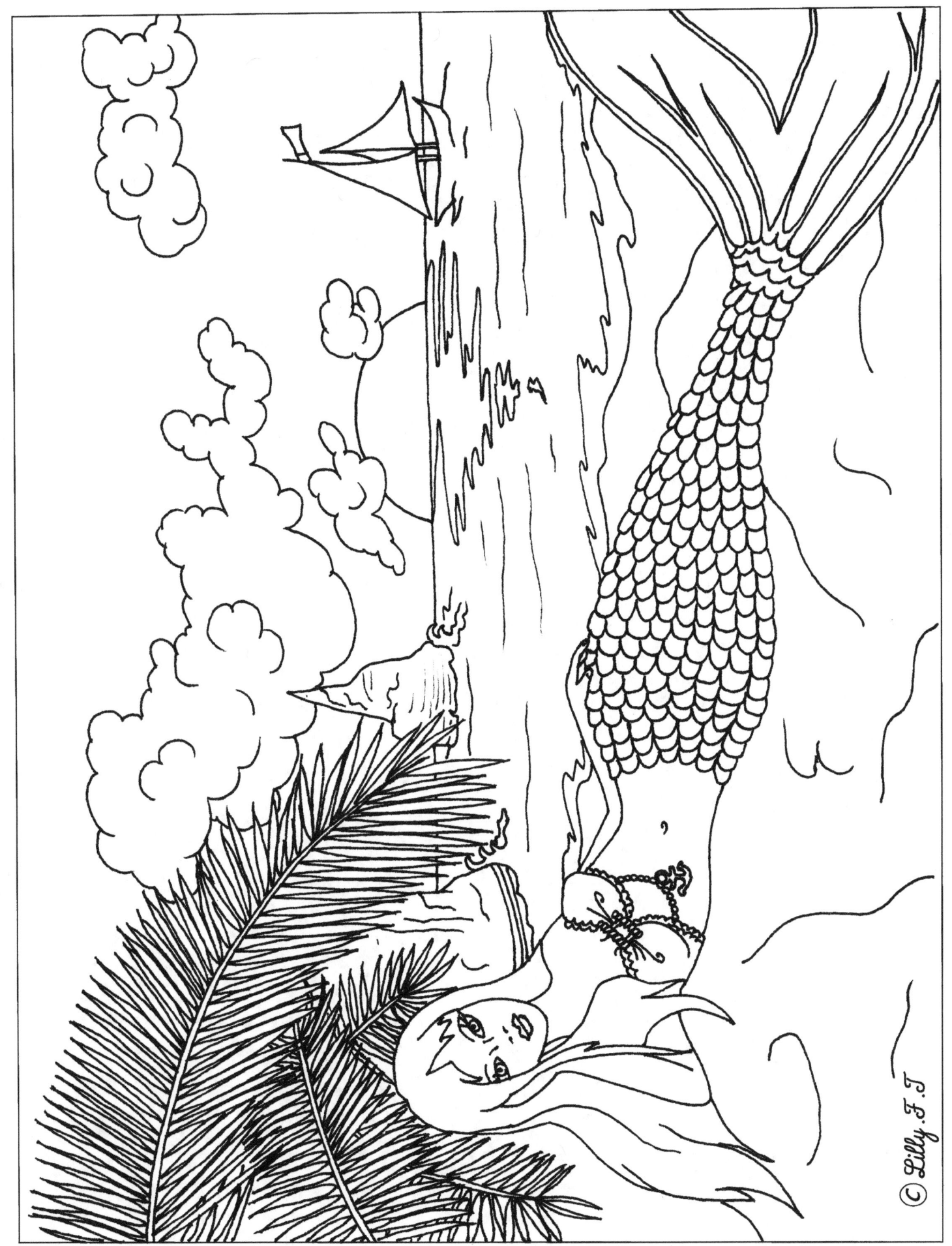

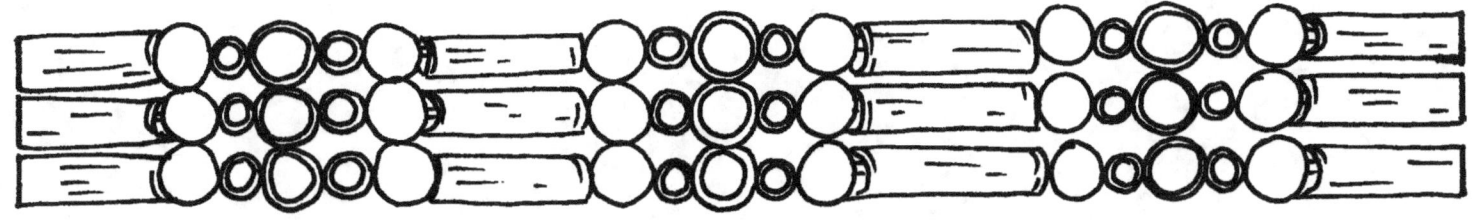

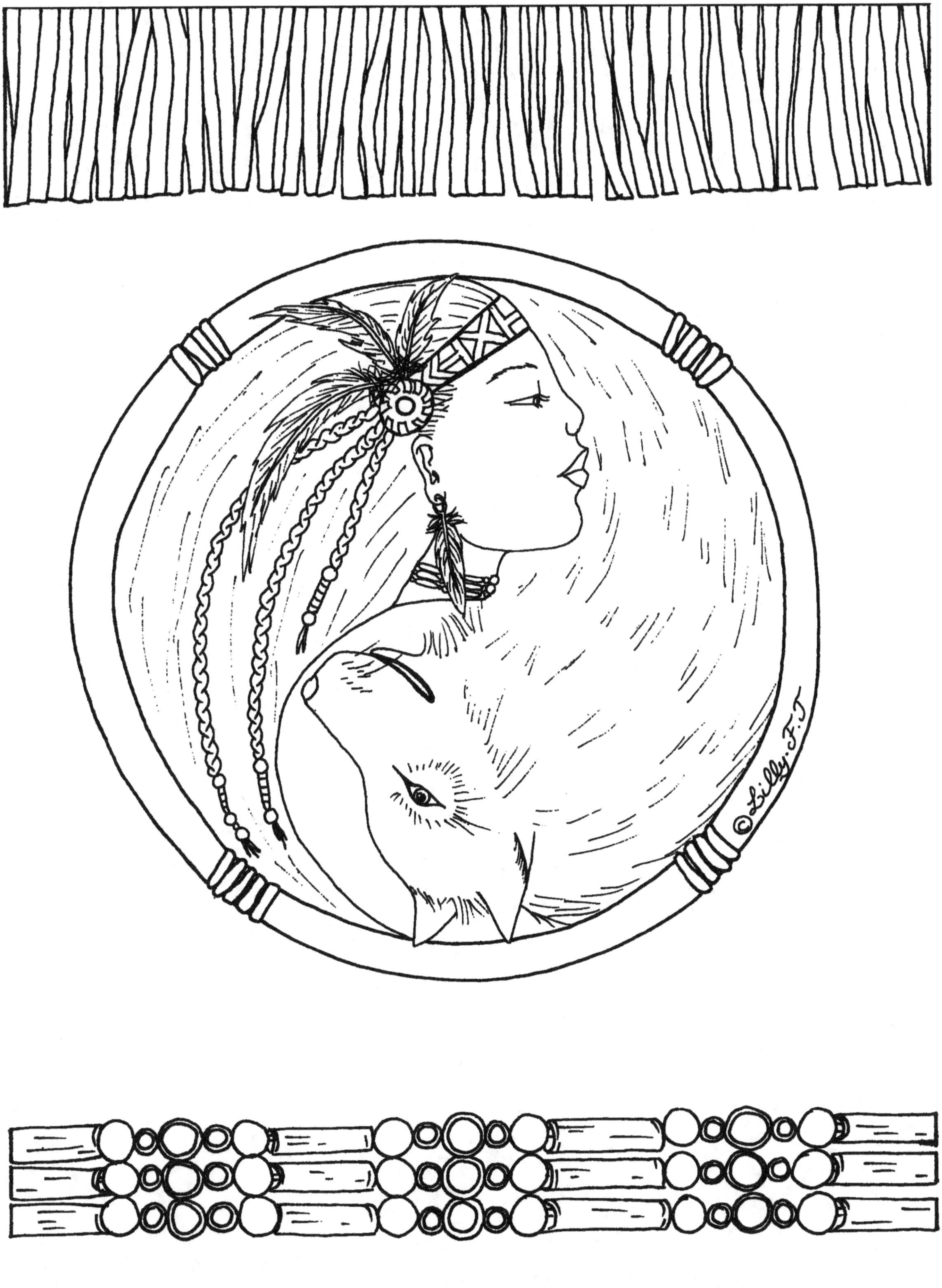

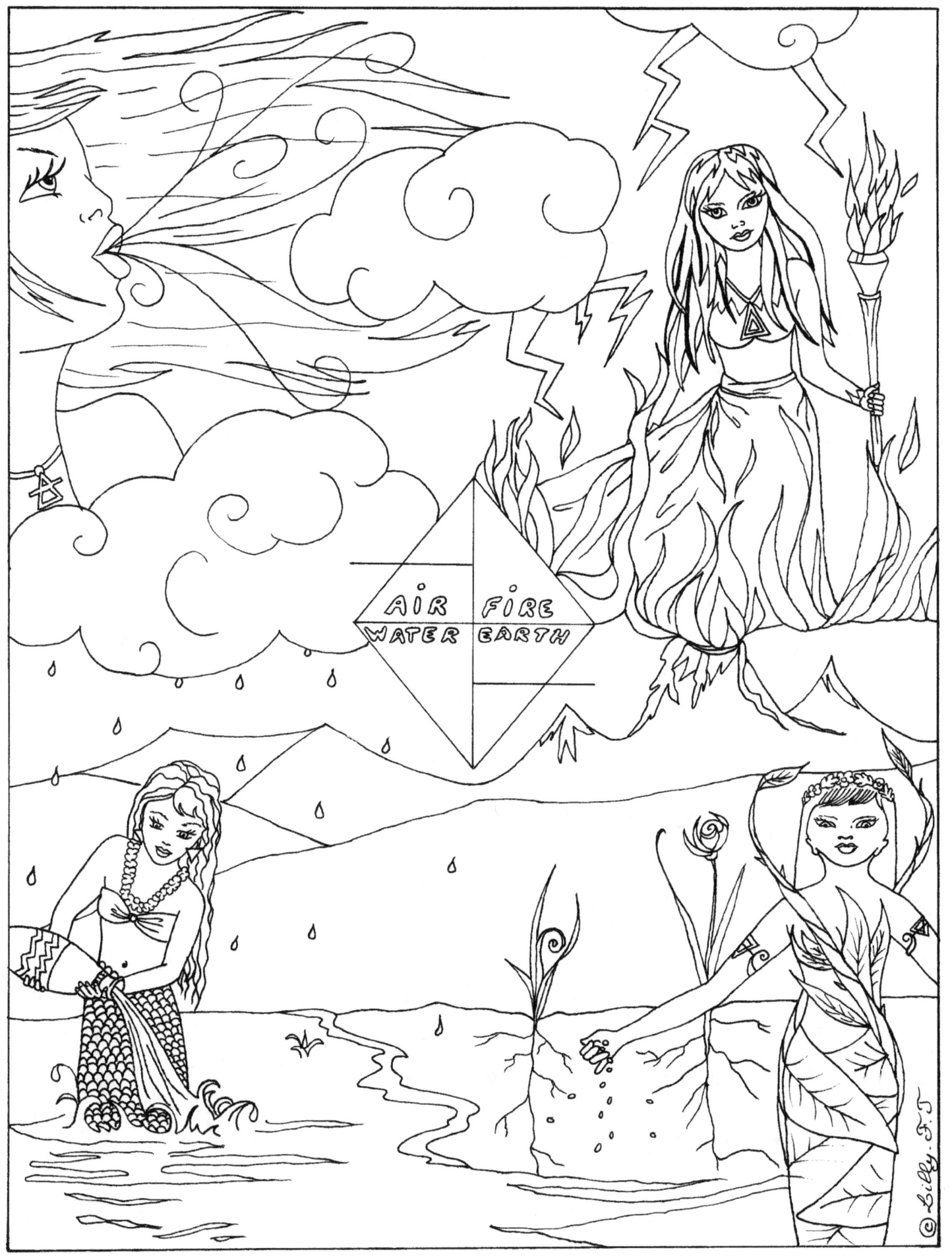

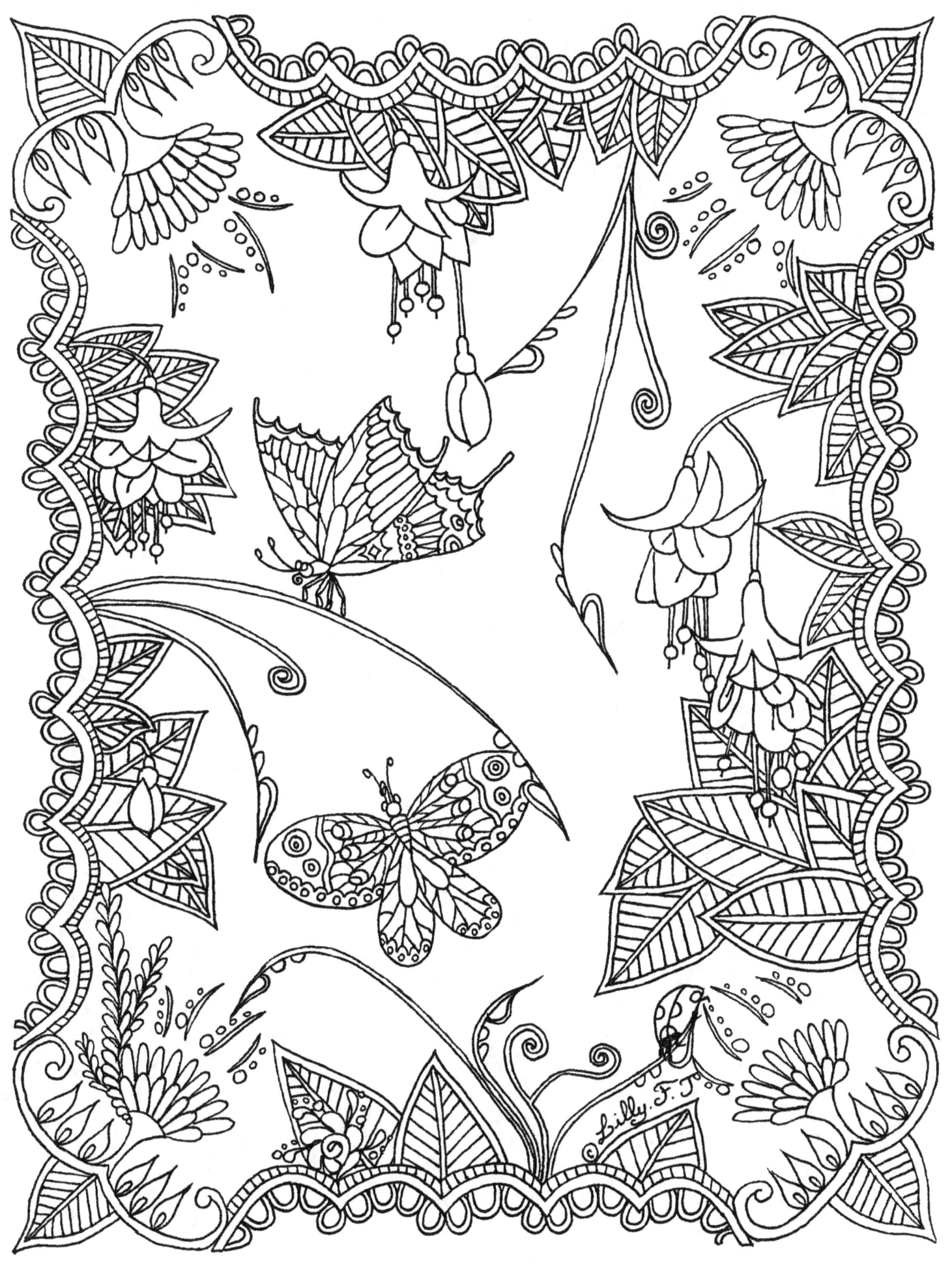

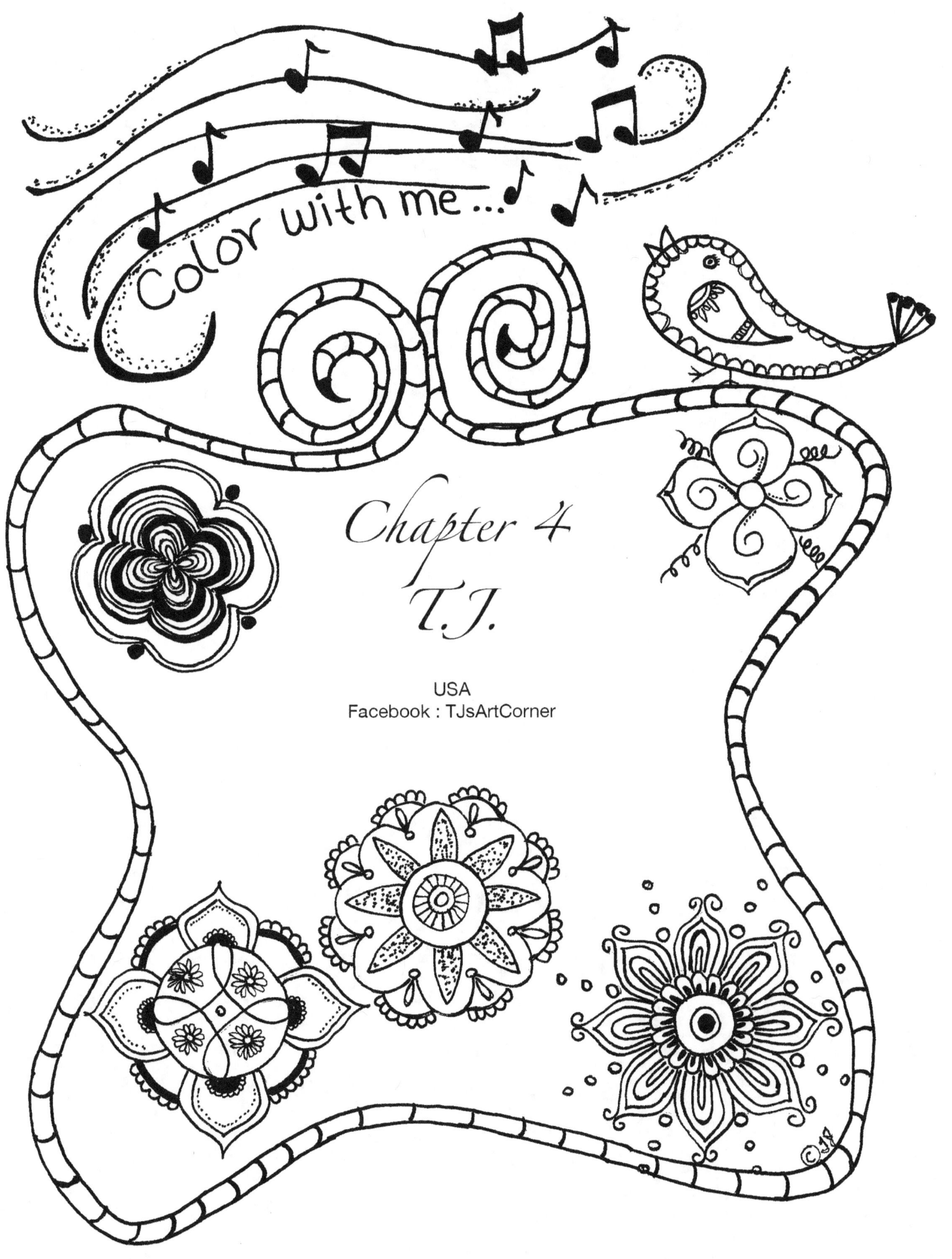

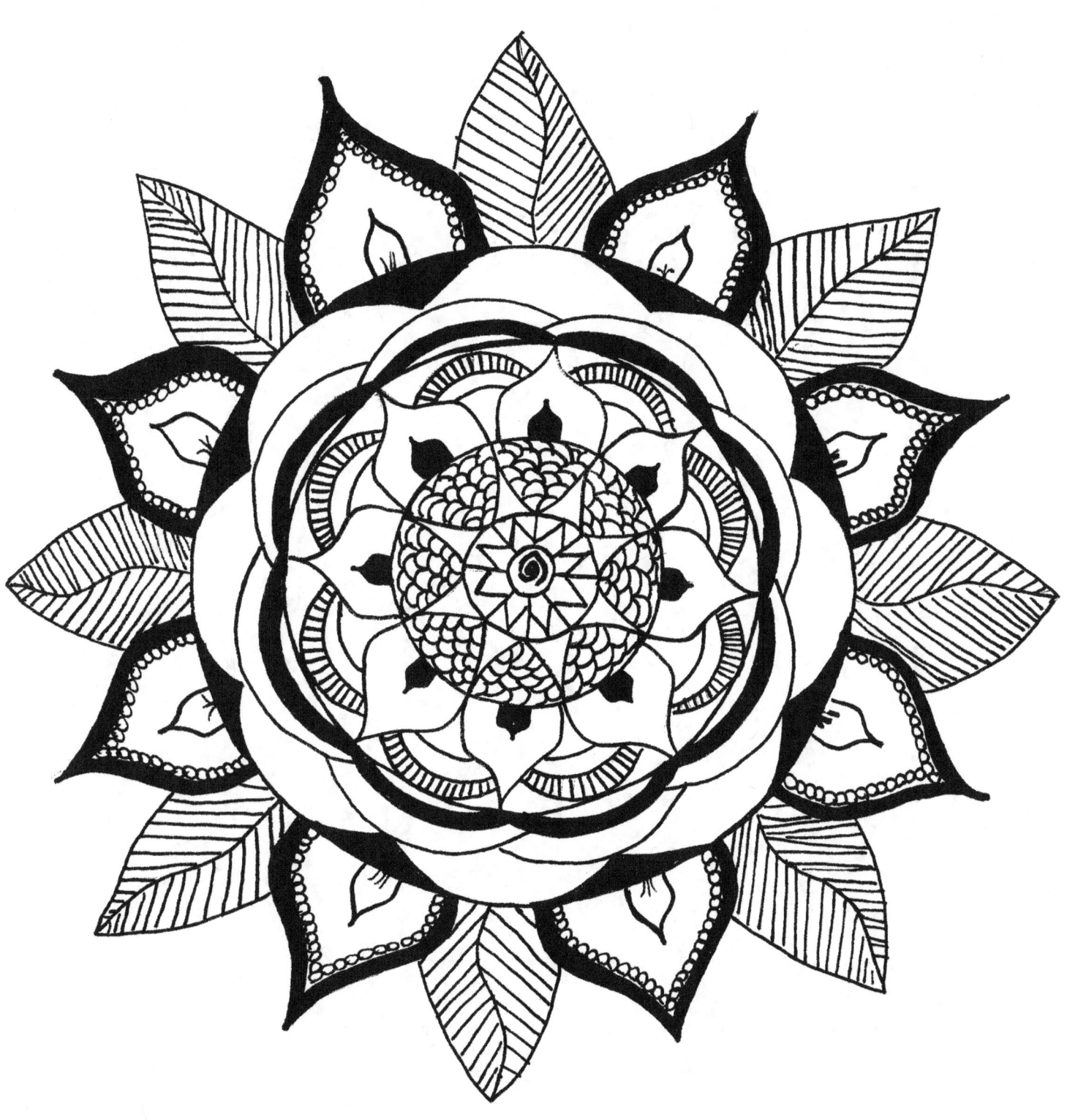

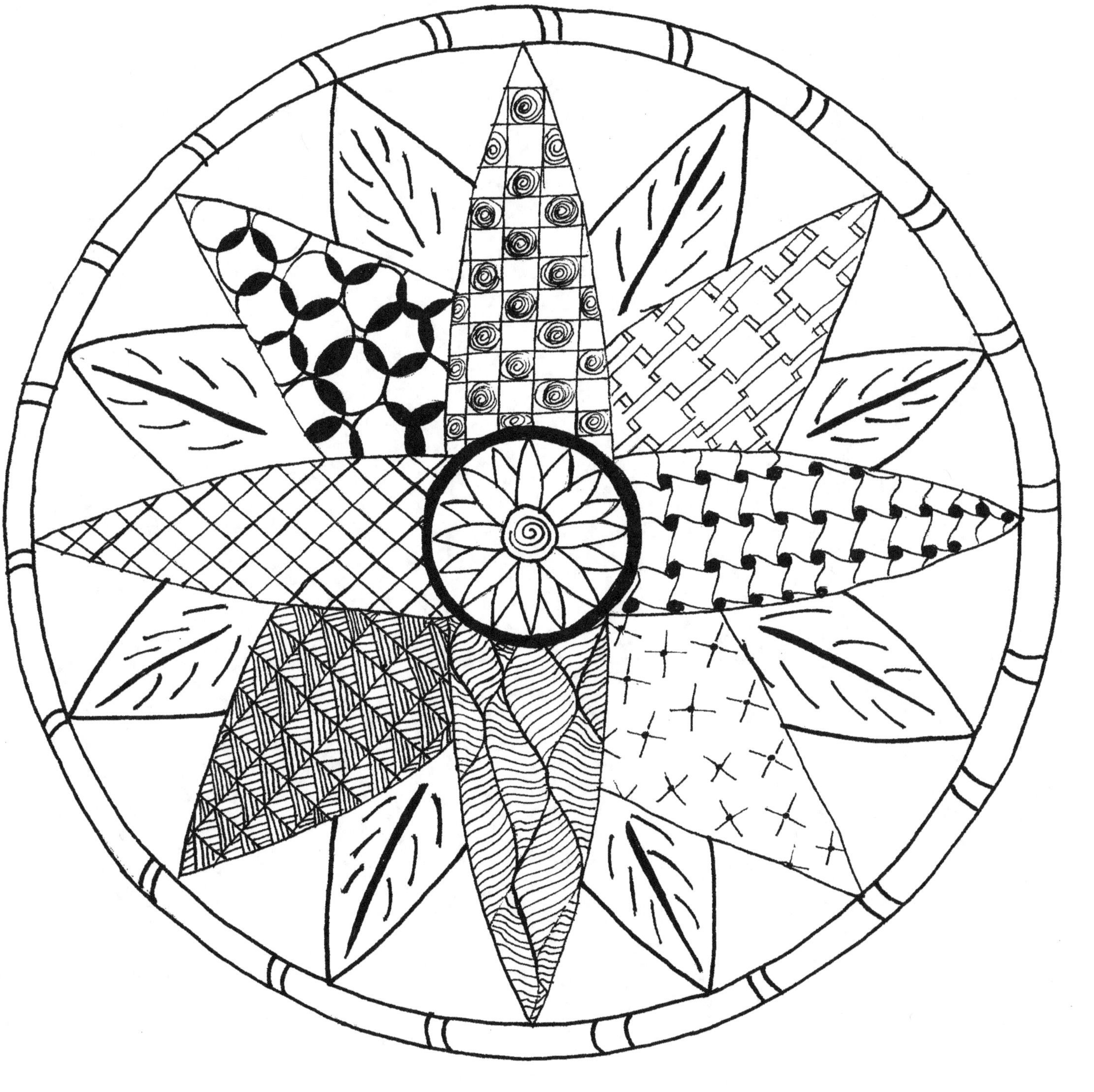

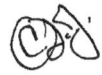

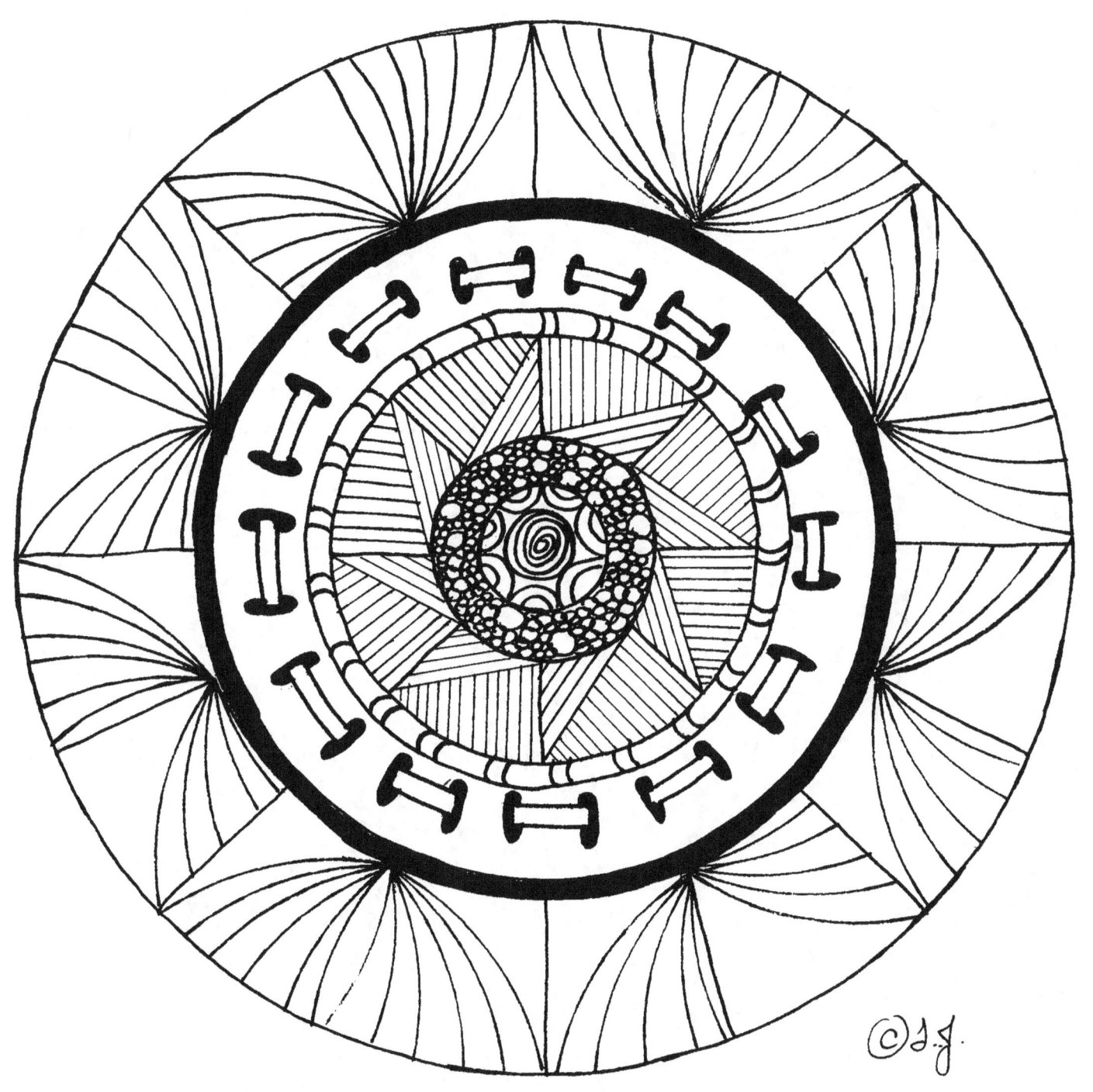

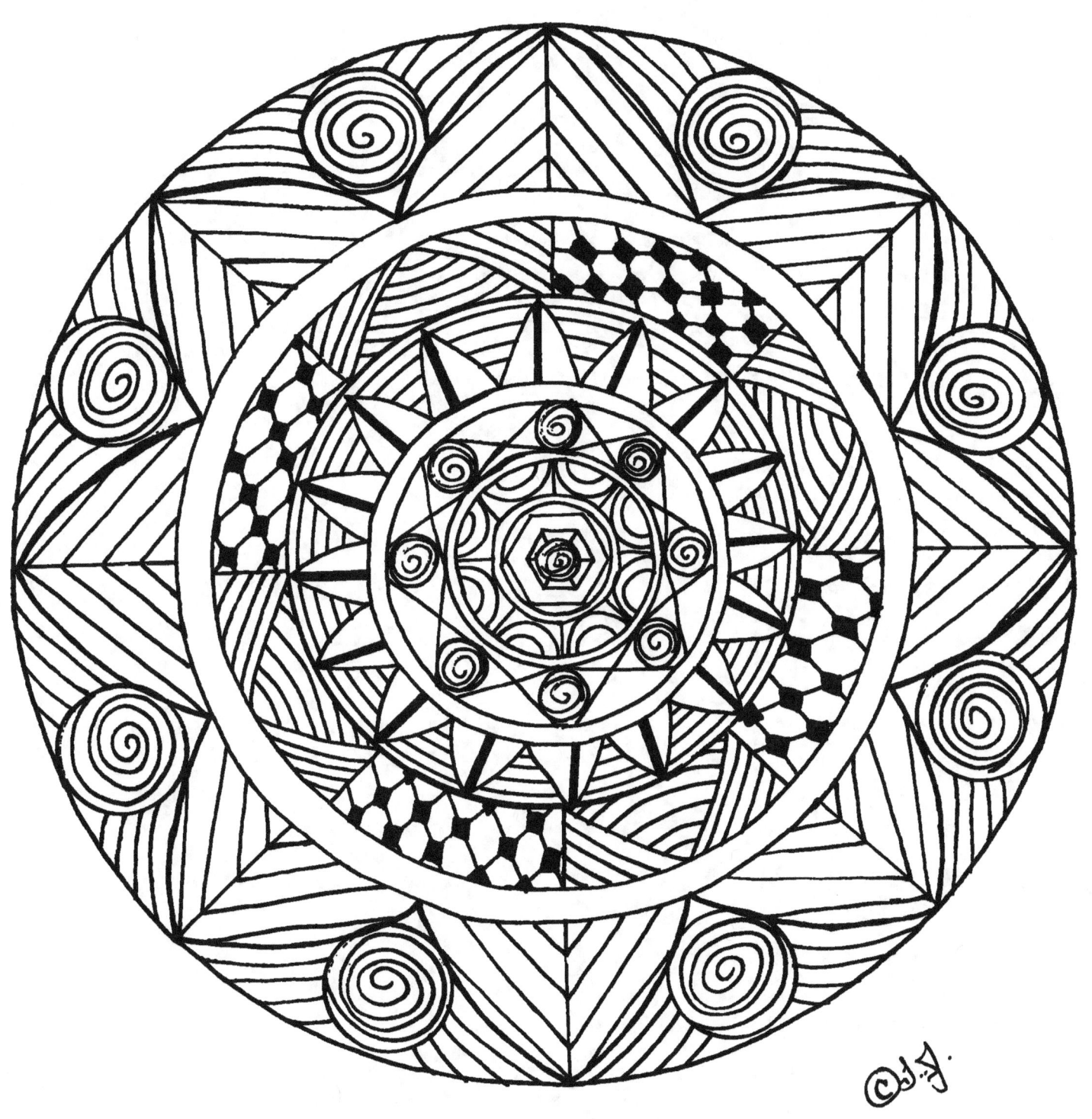

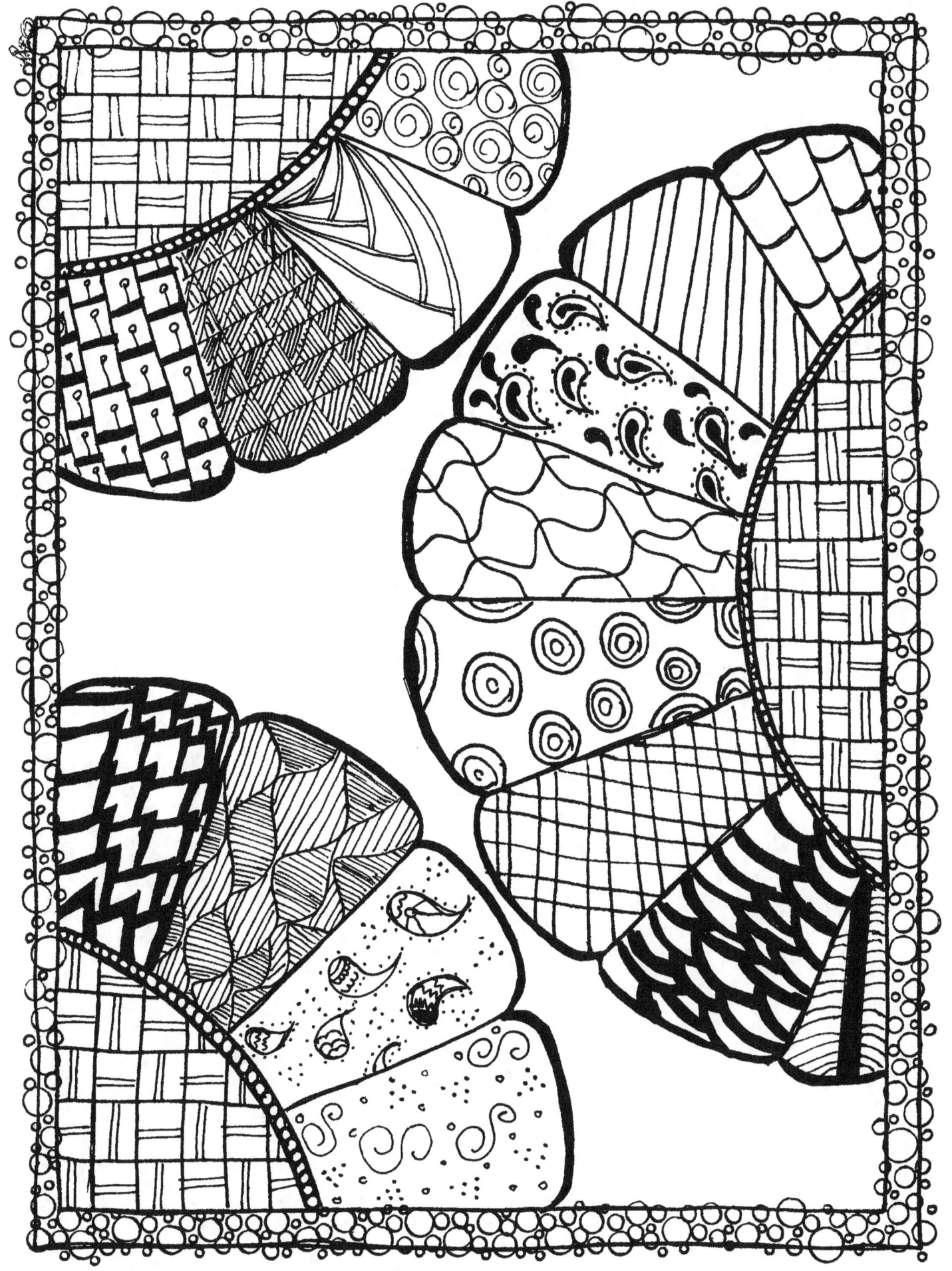

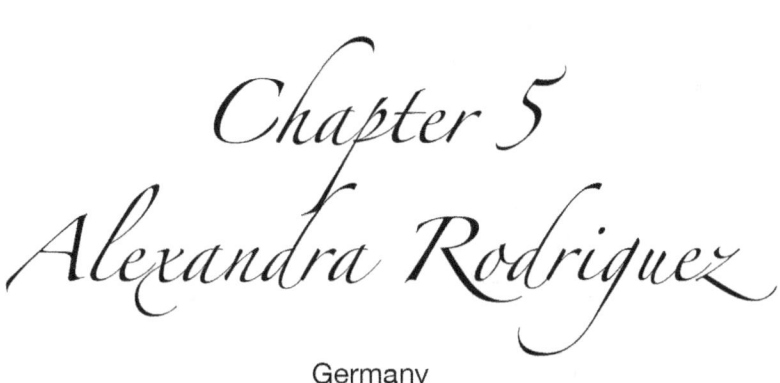

Chapter 5
Alexandra Rodriguez

Germany

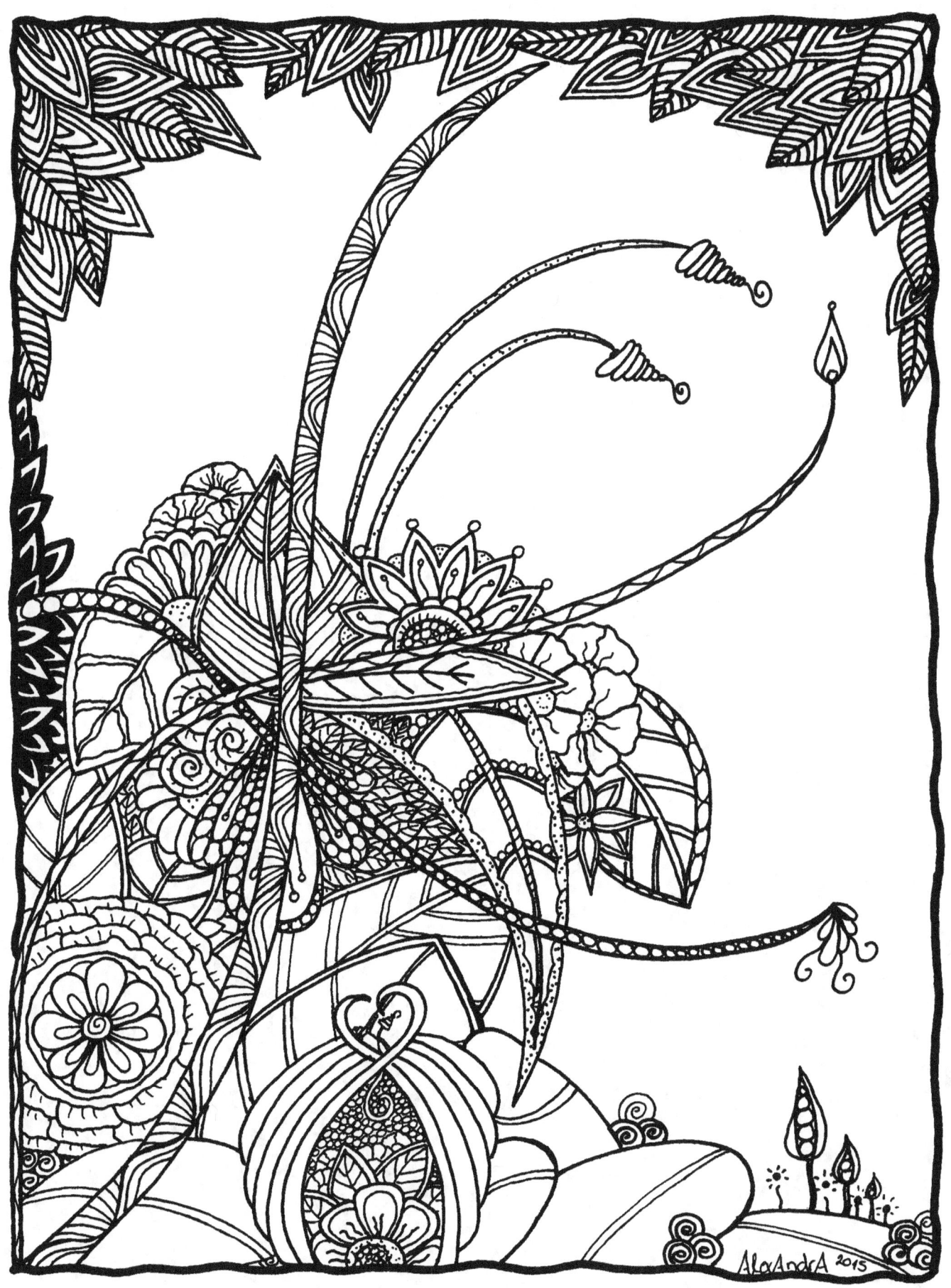

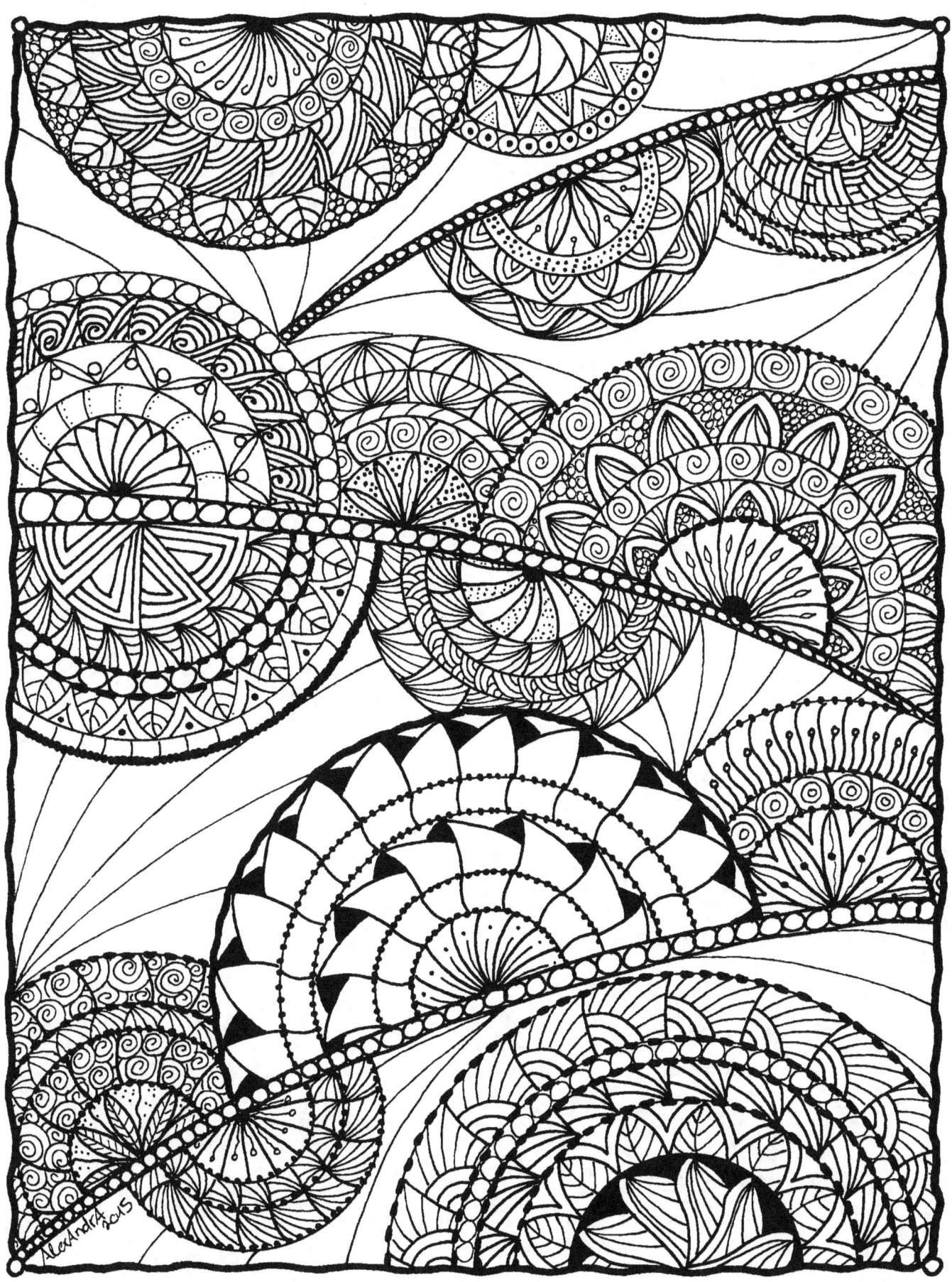

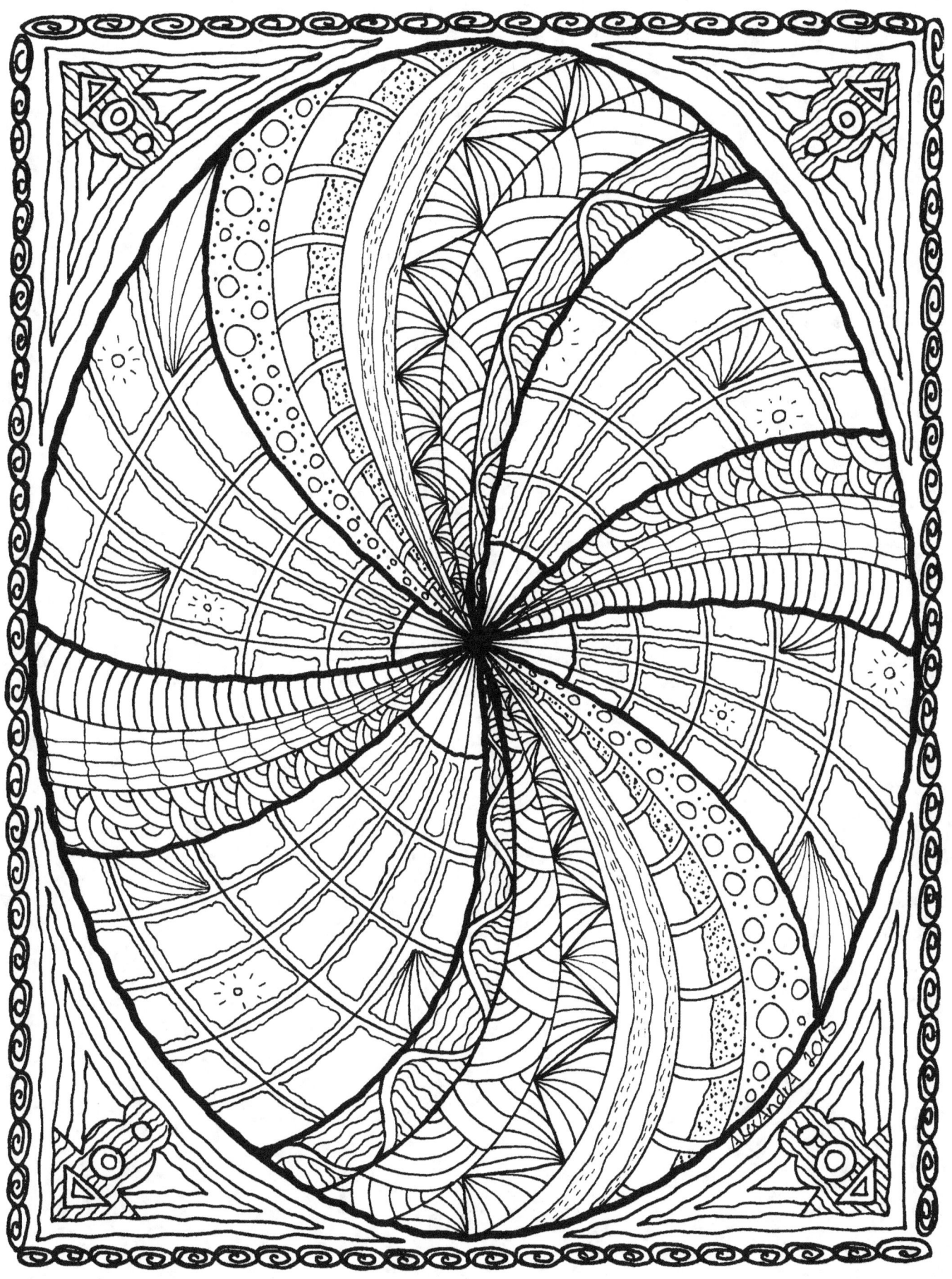

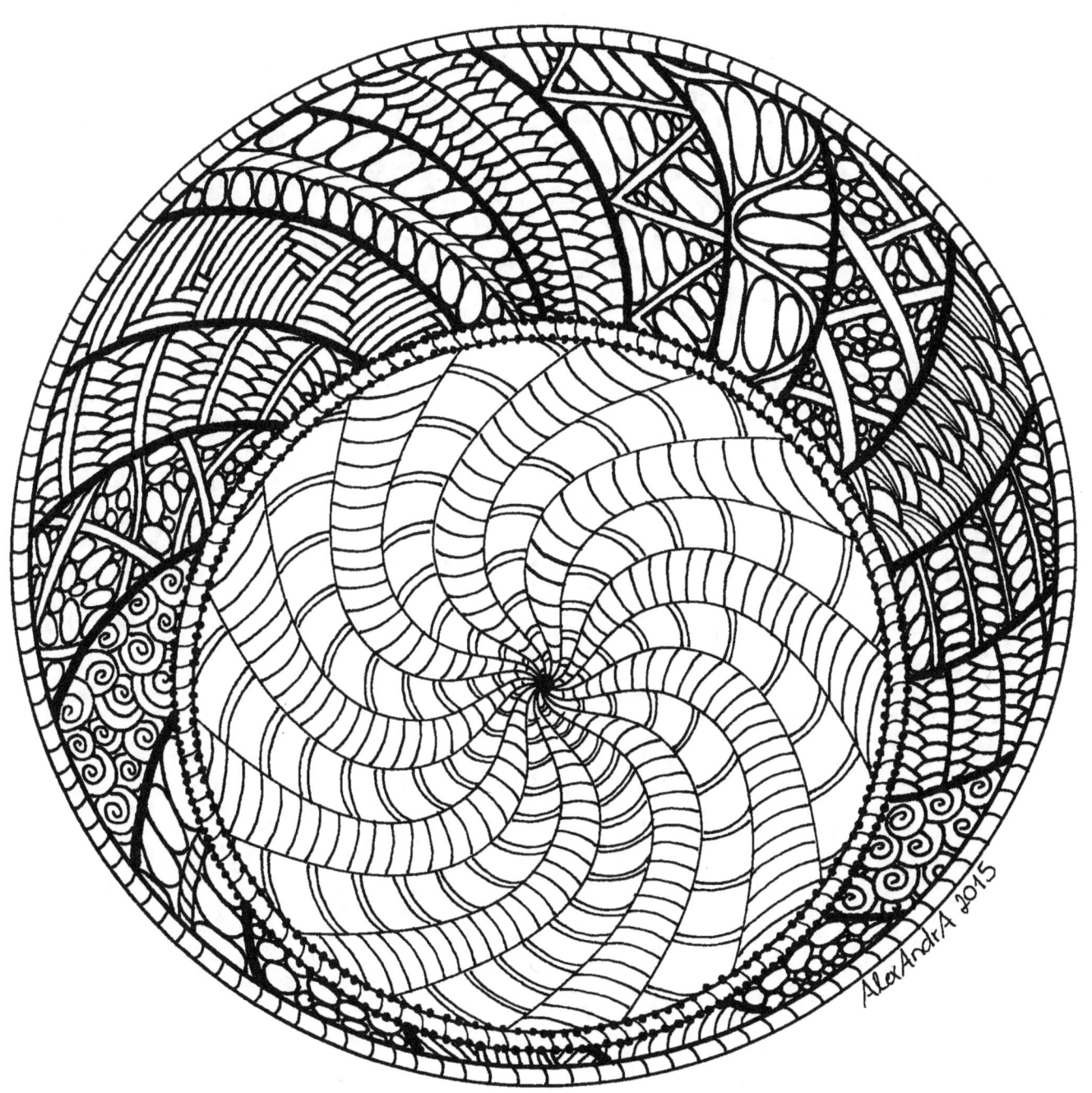

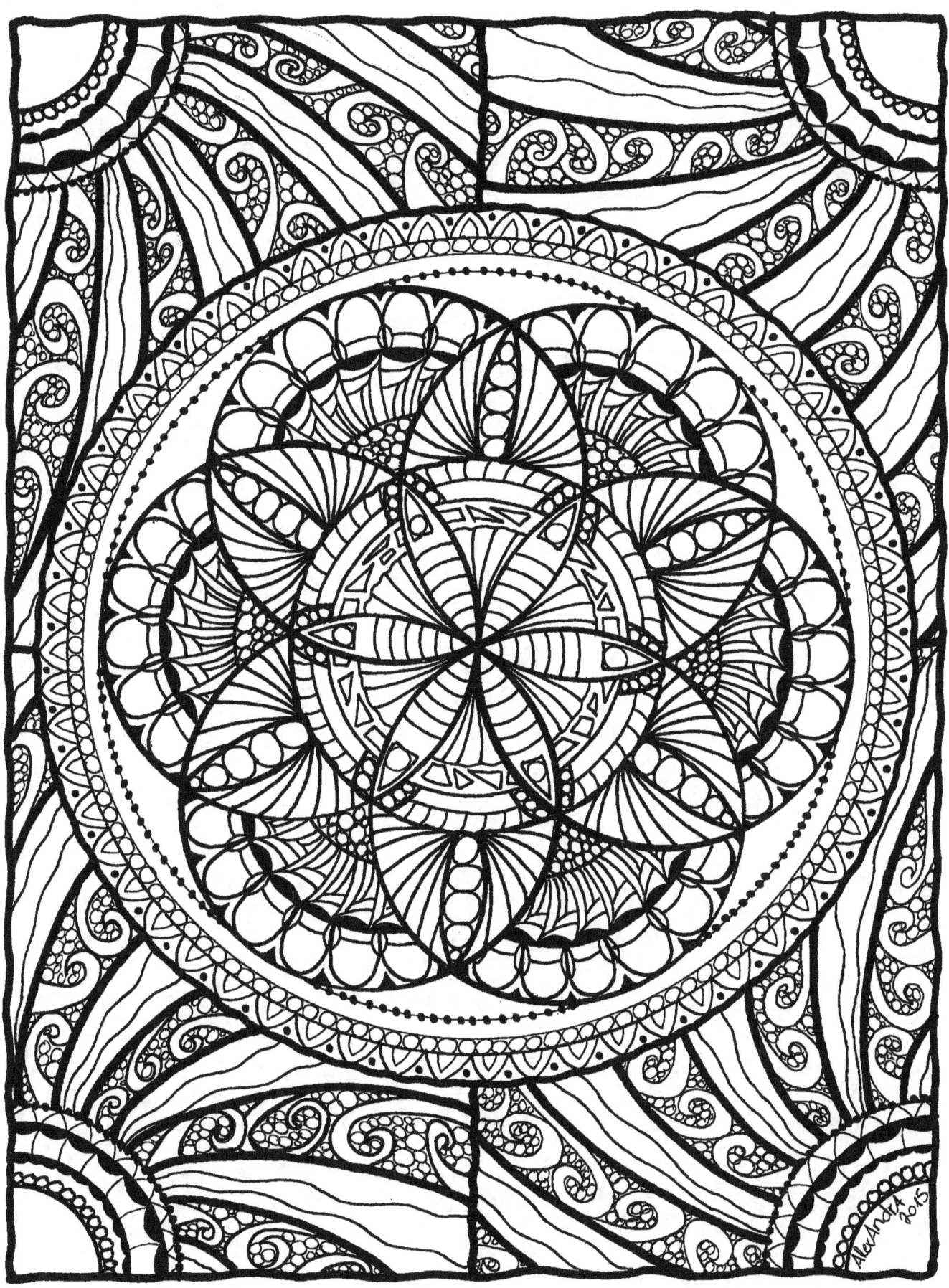

Chapter 6
Gloria A. Lenzen

USA

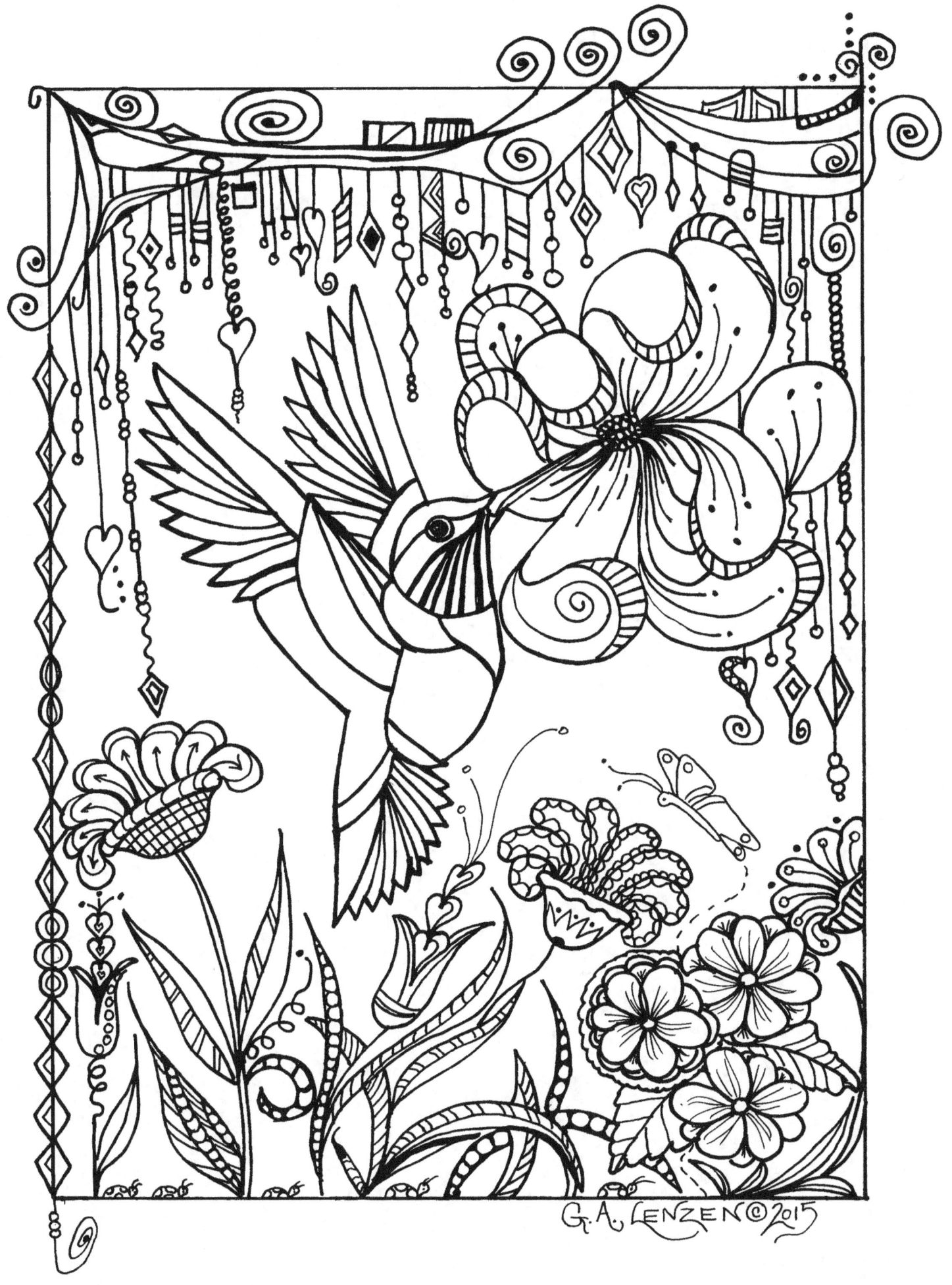

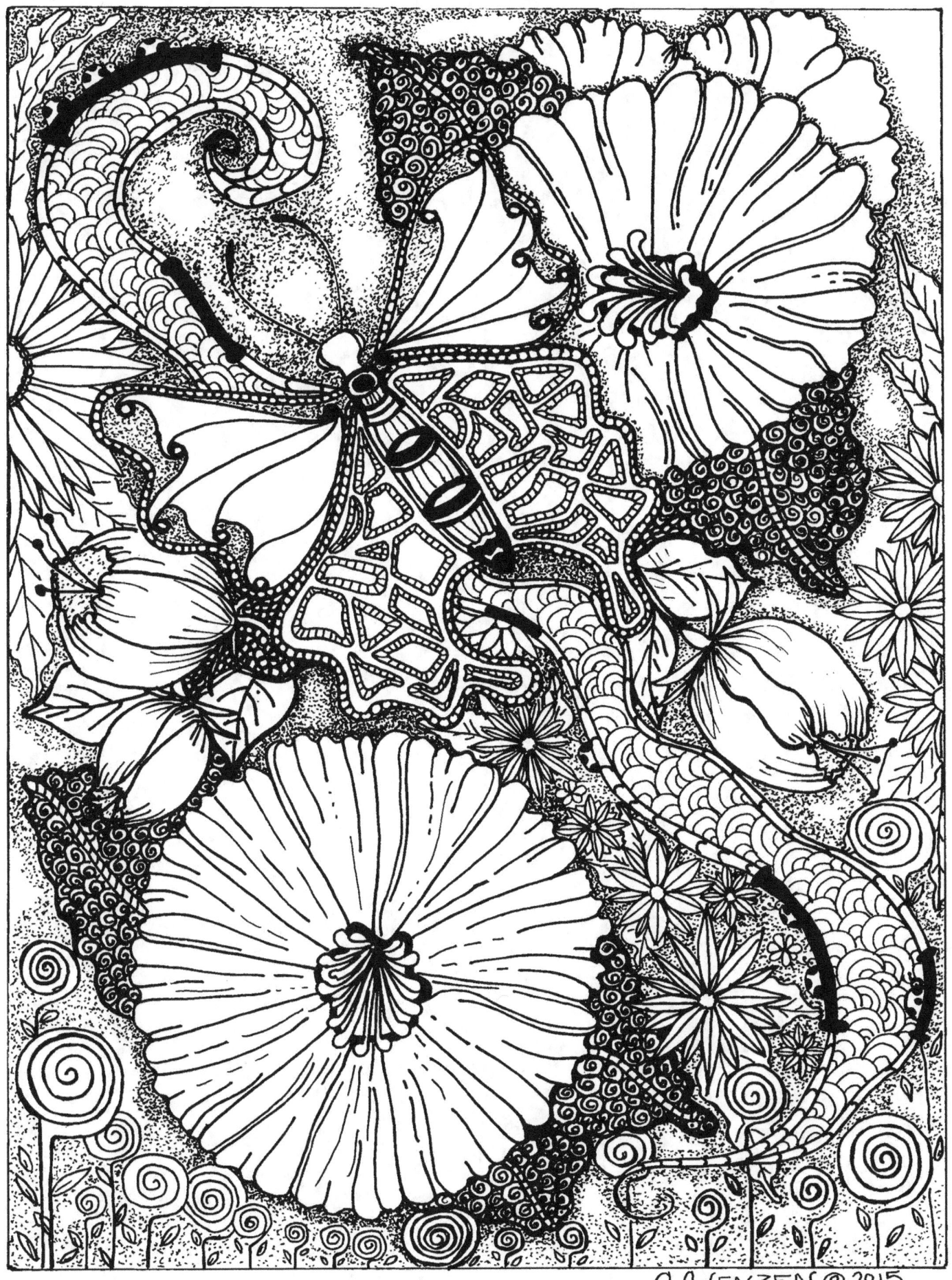

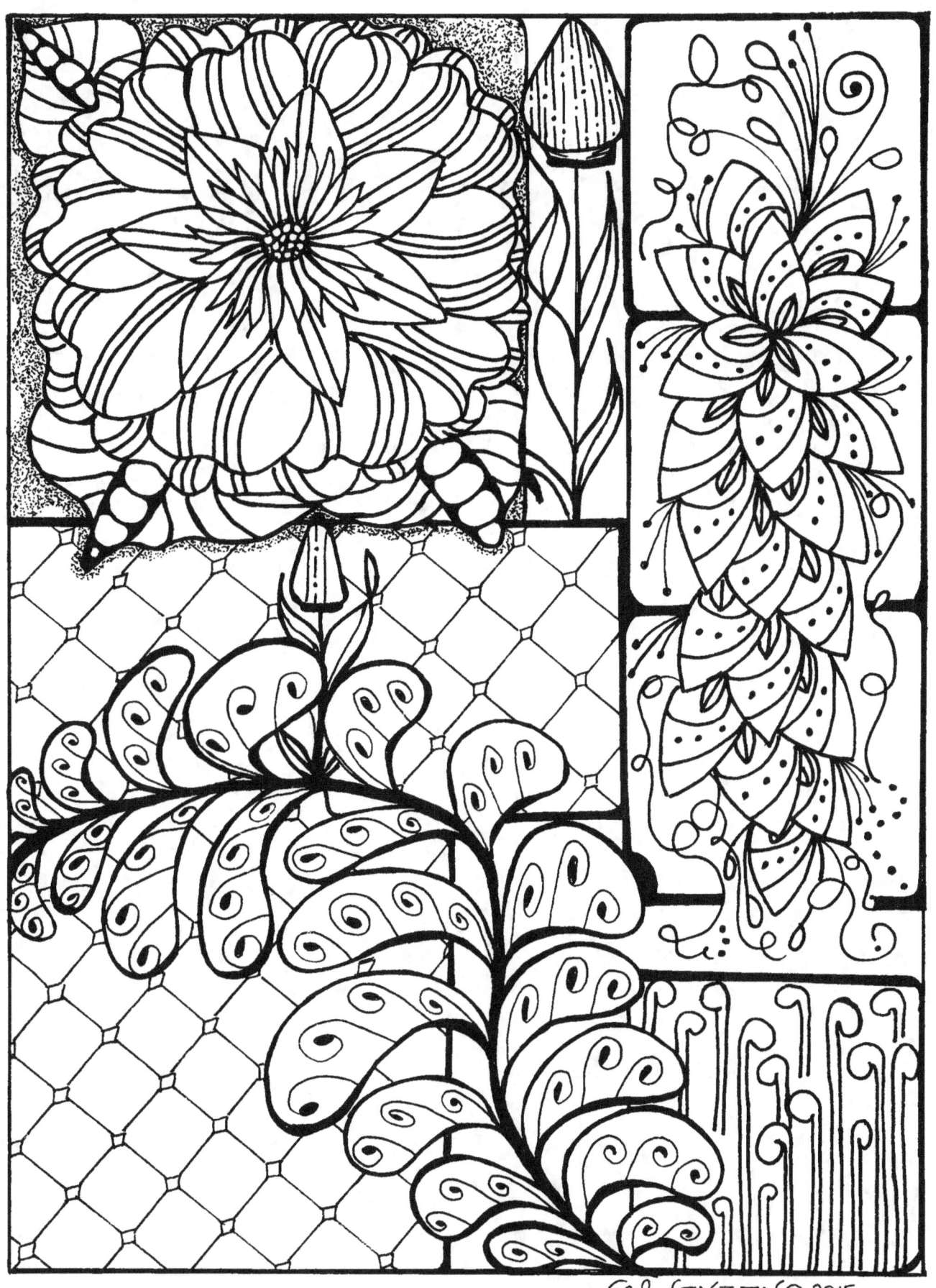

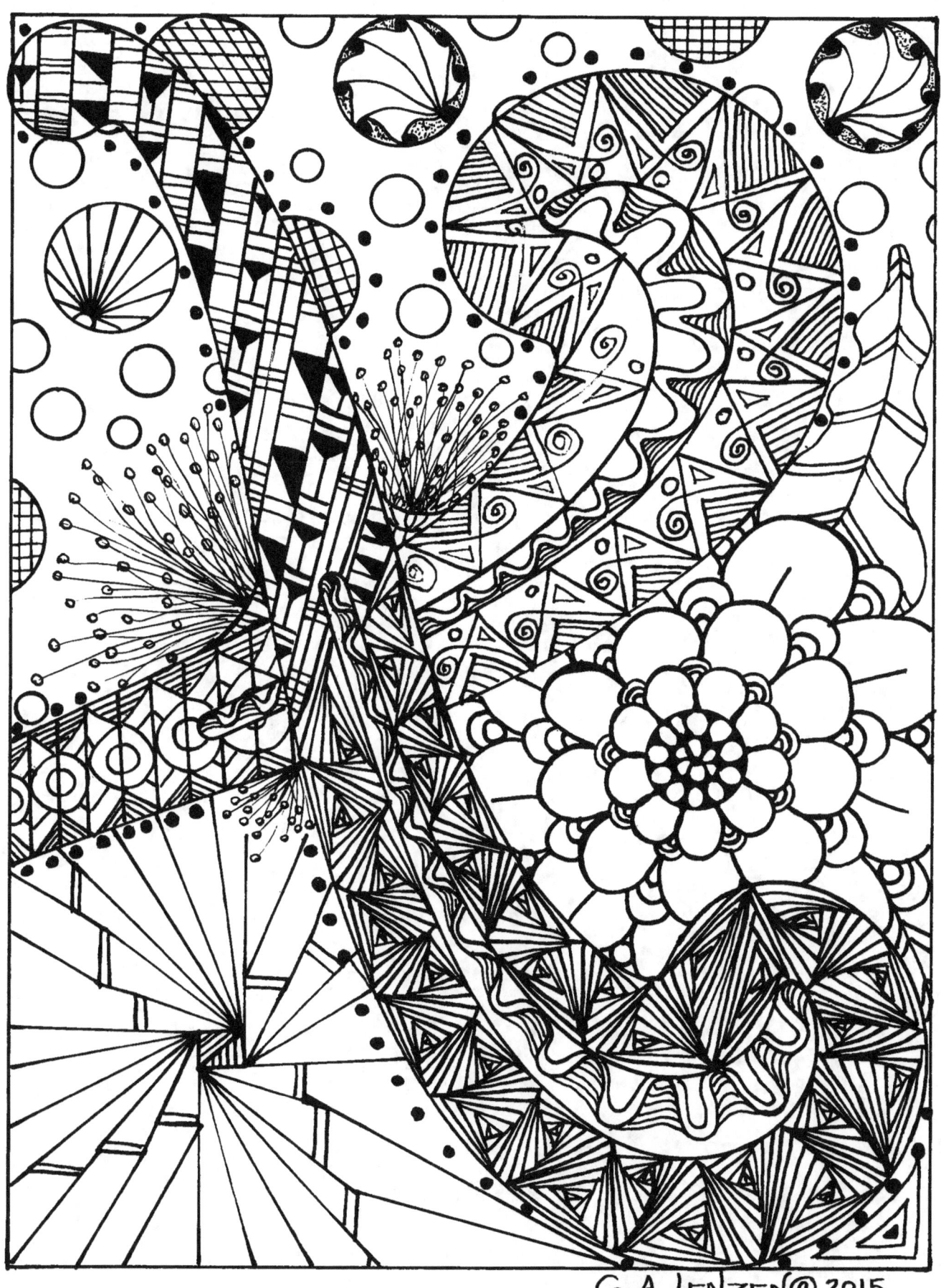

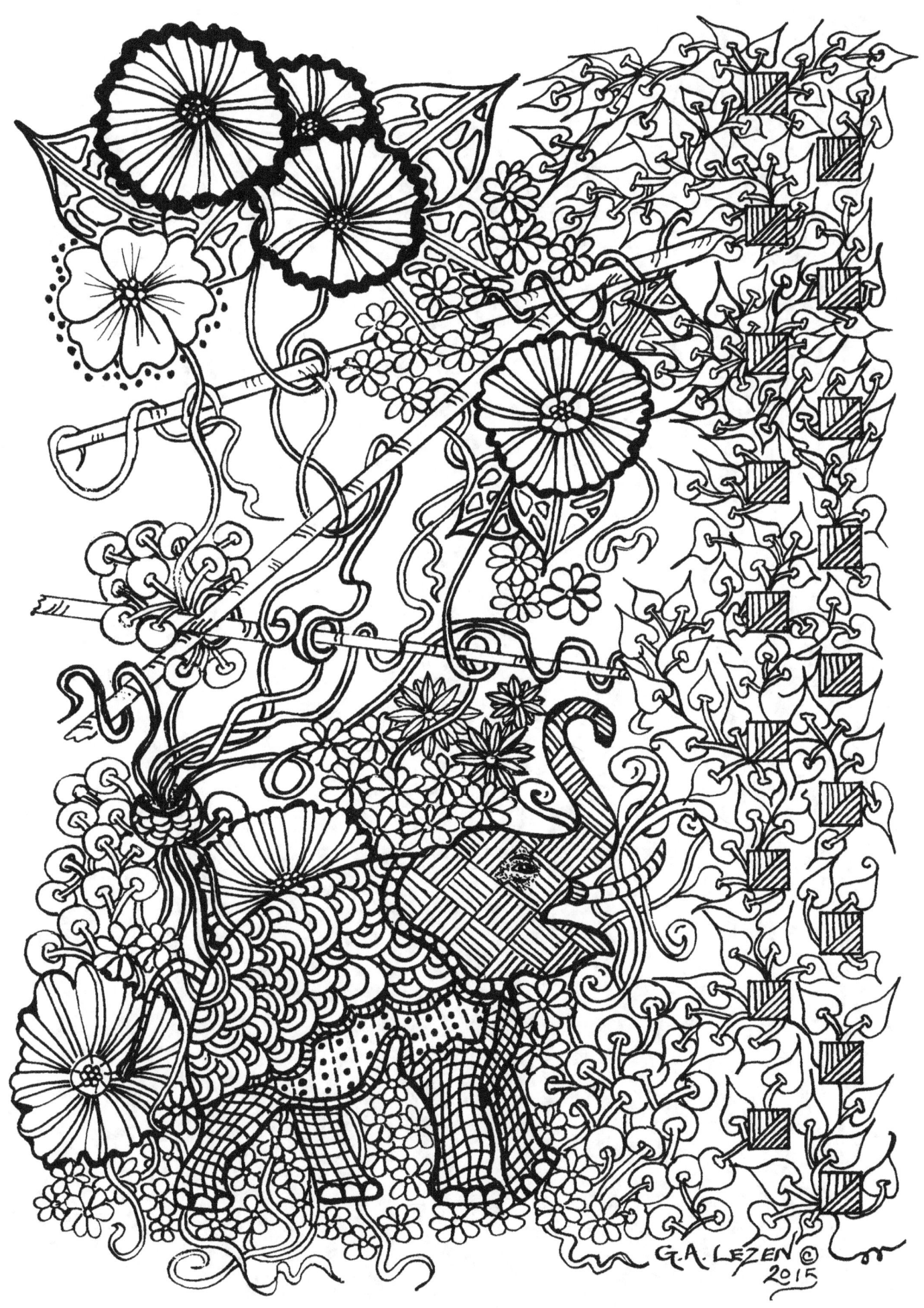

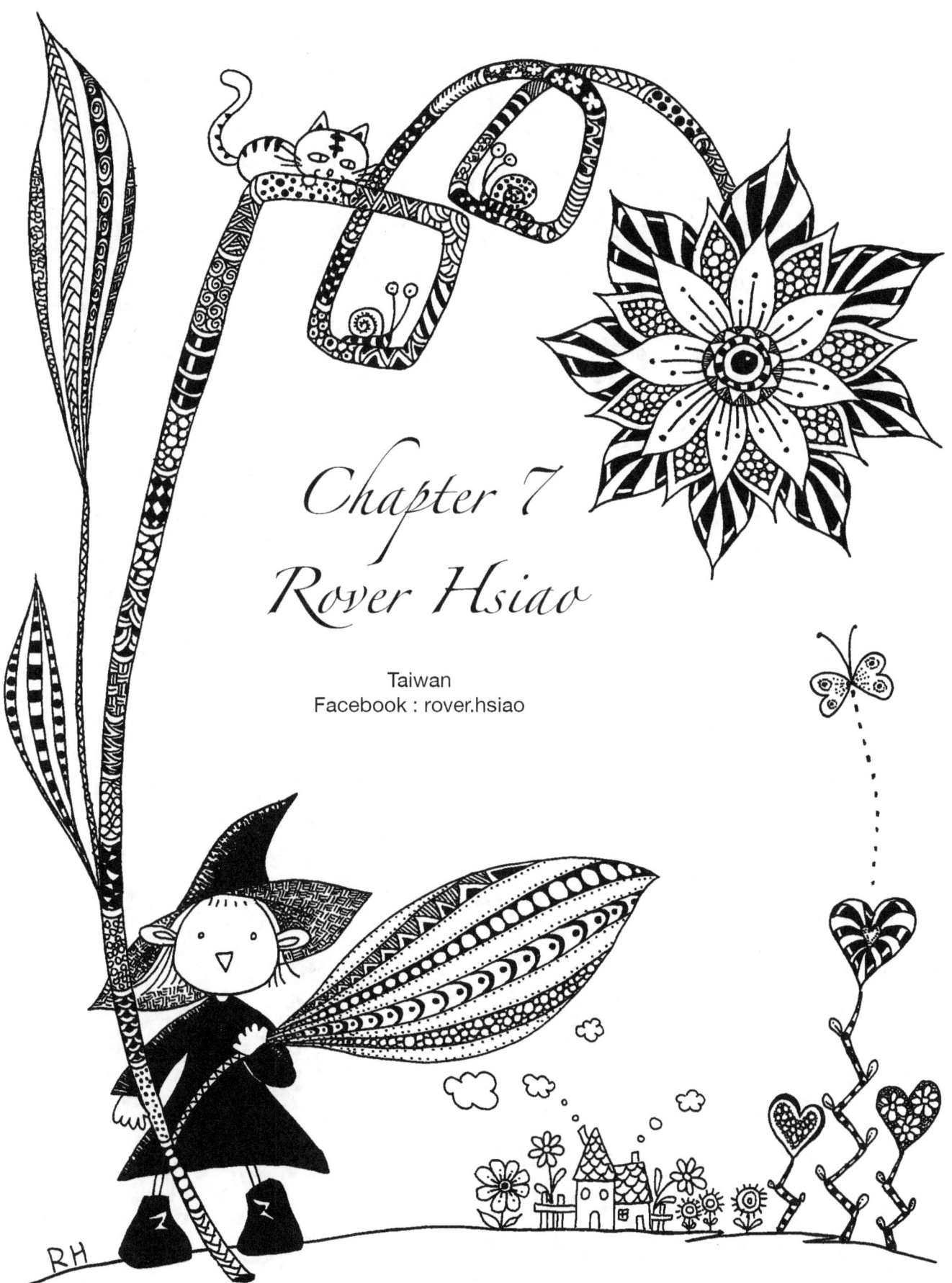

Chapter 7
Rover Hsiao

Taiwan
Facebook : rover.hsiao

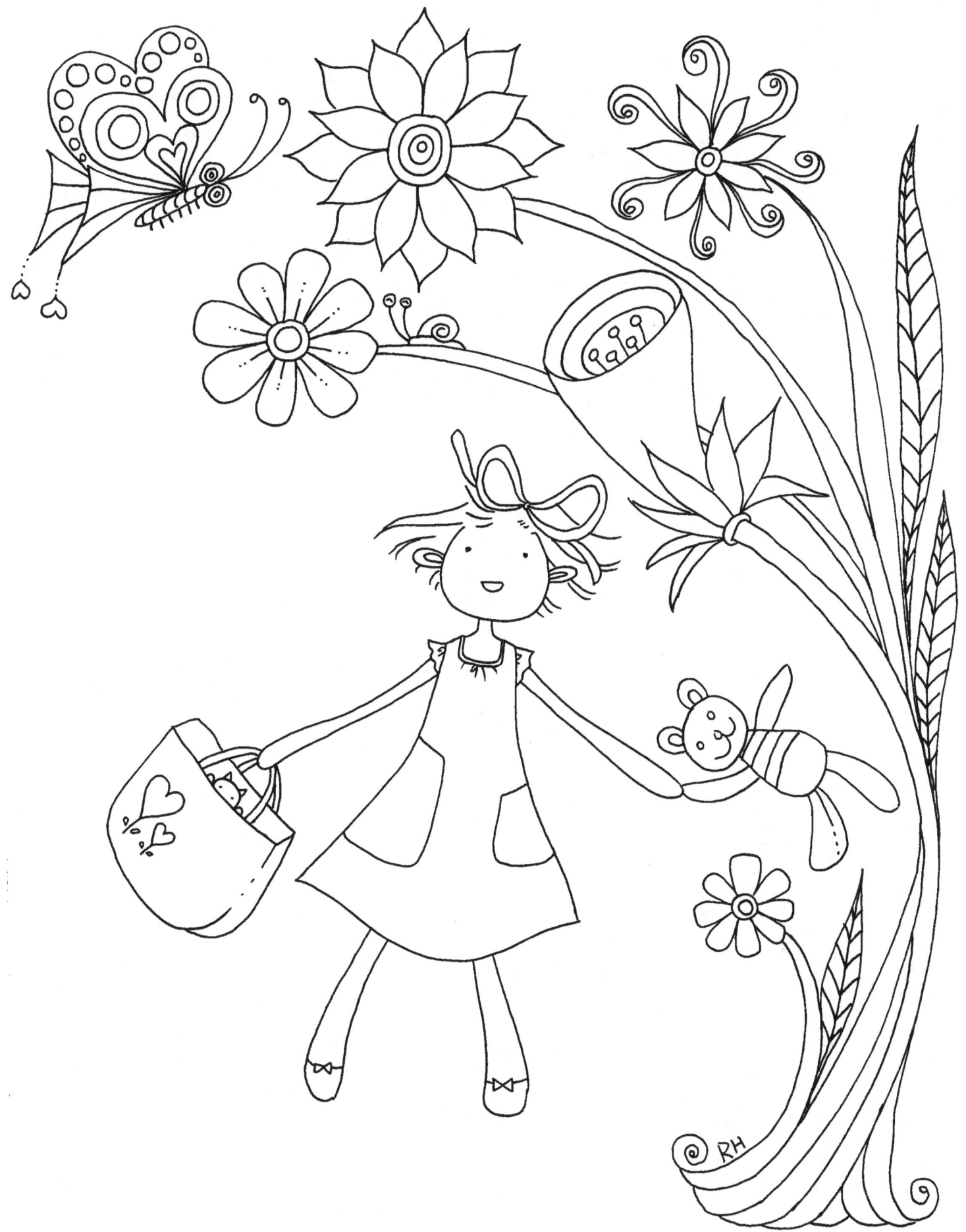

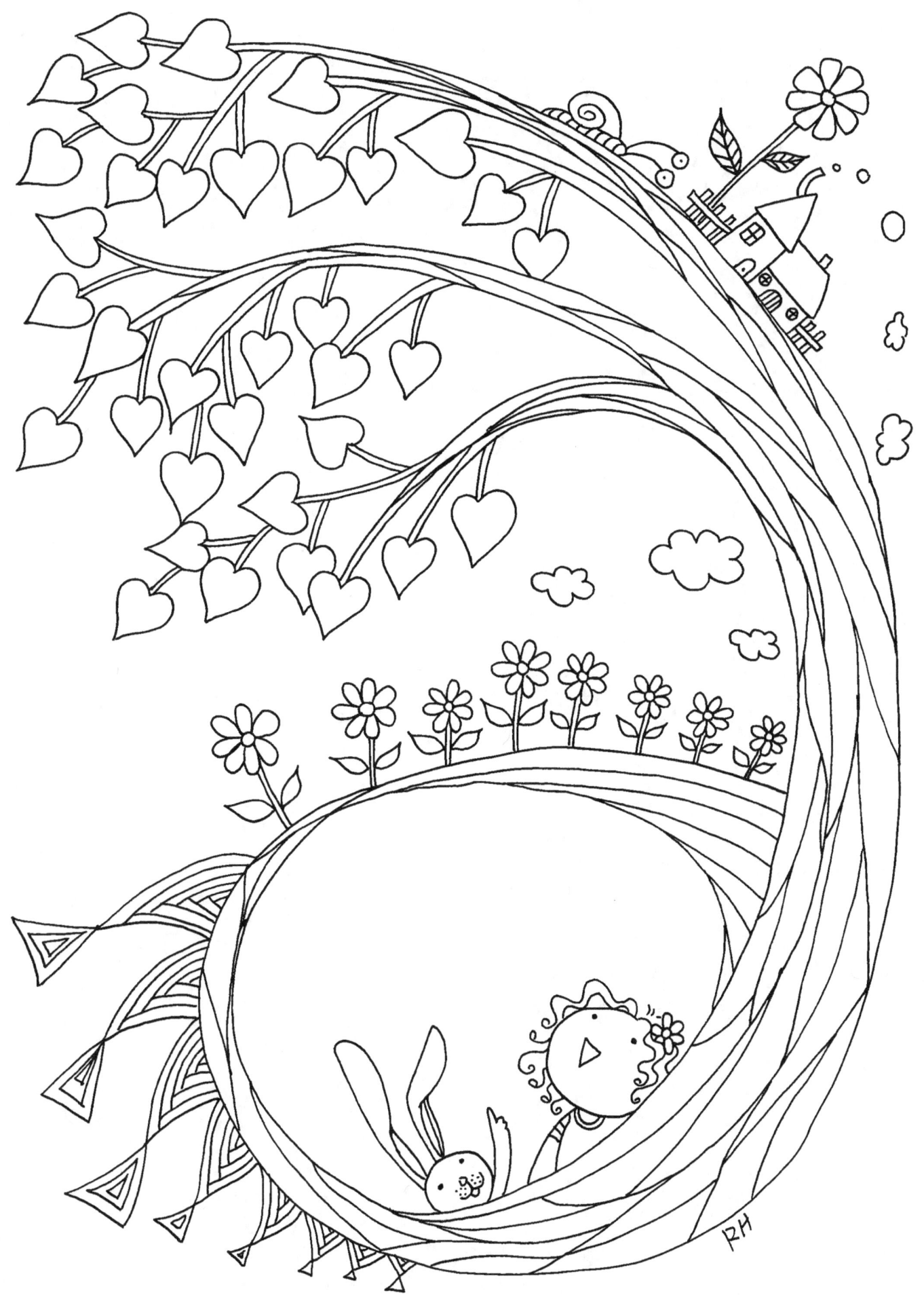

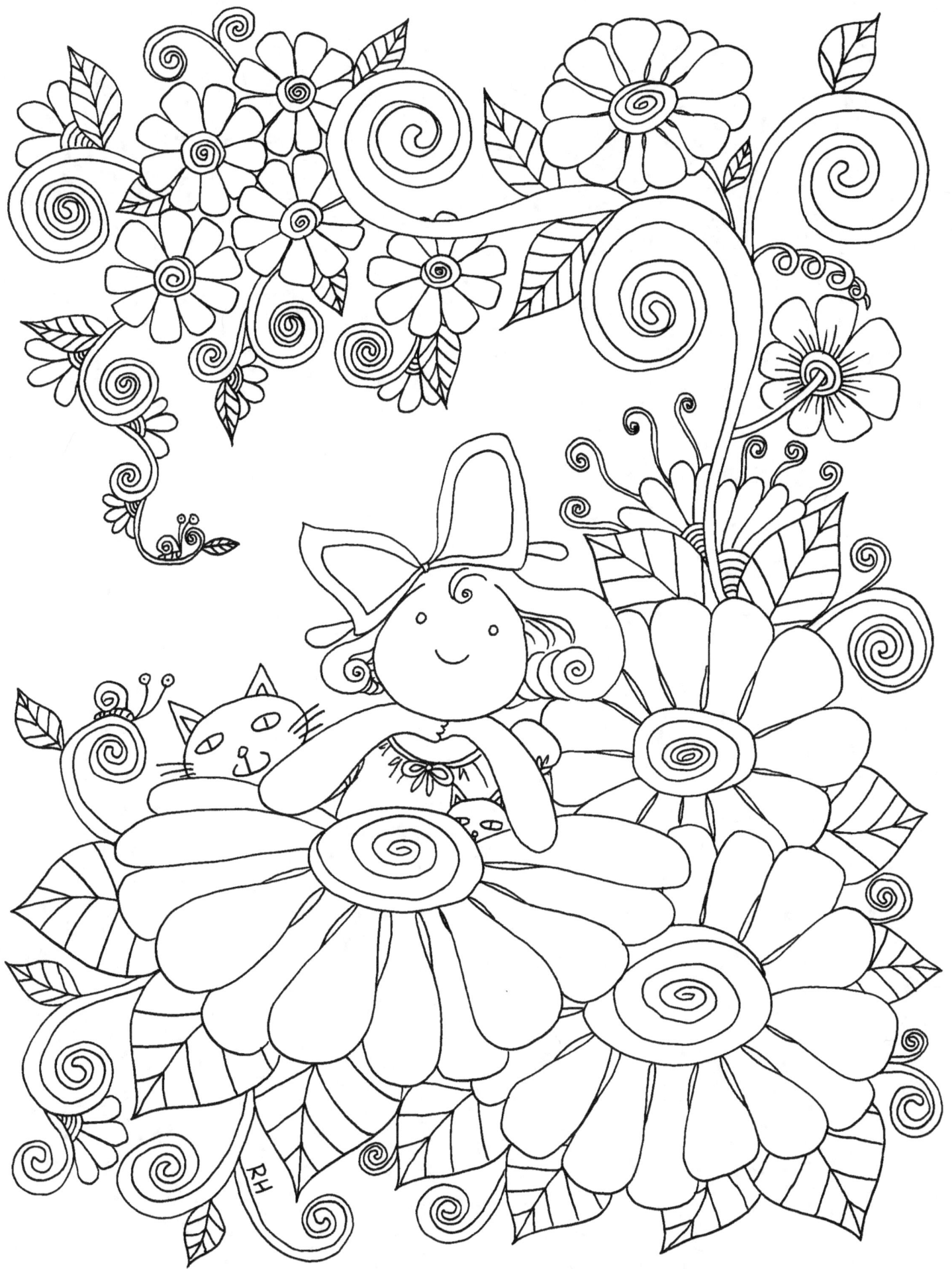

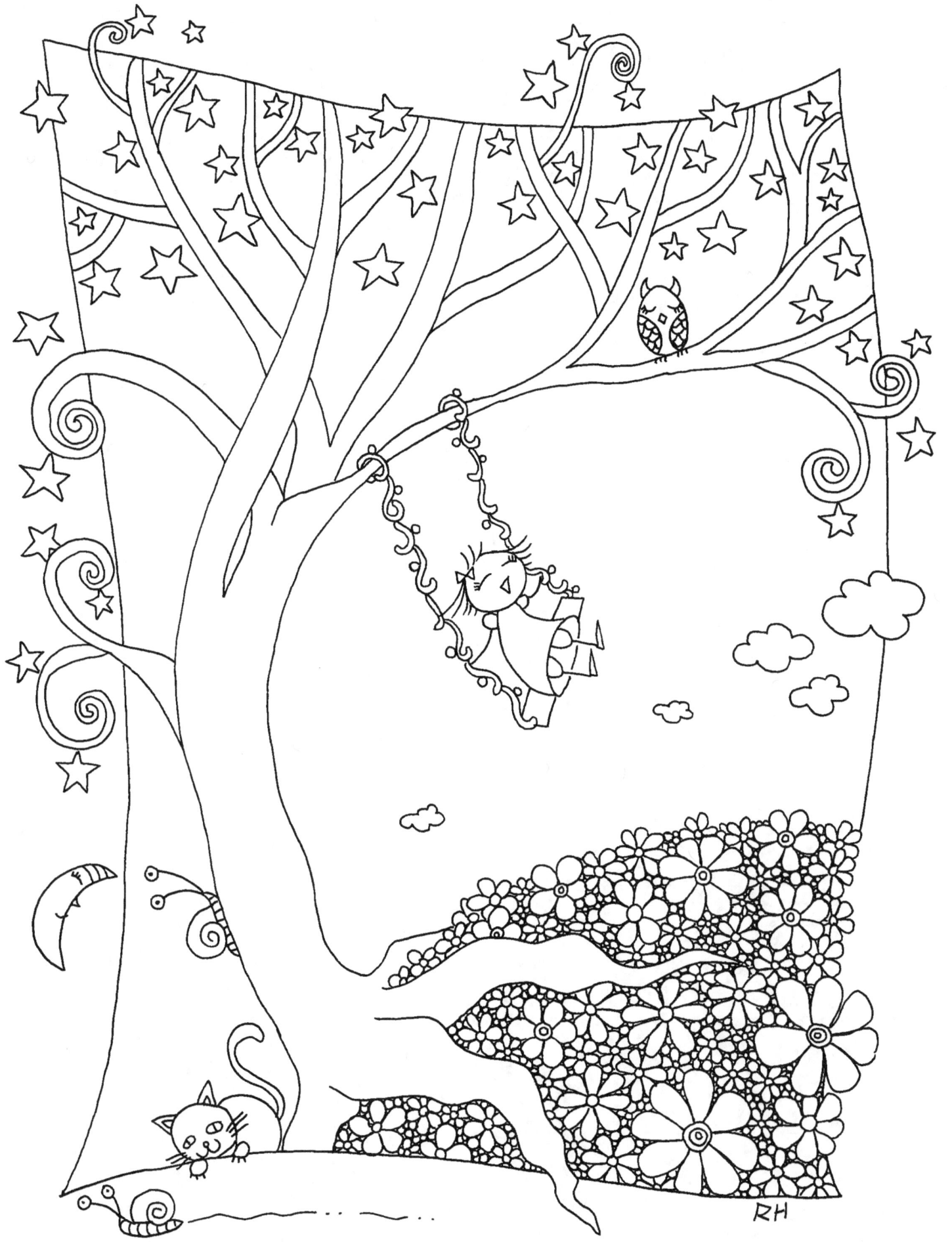

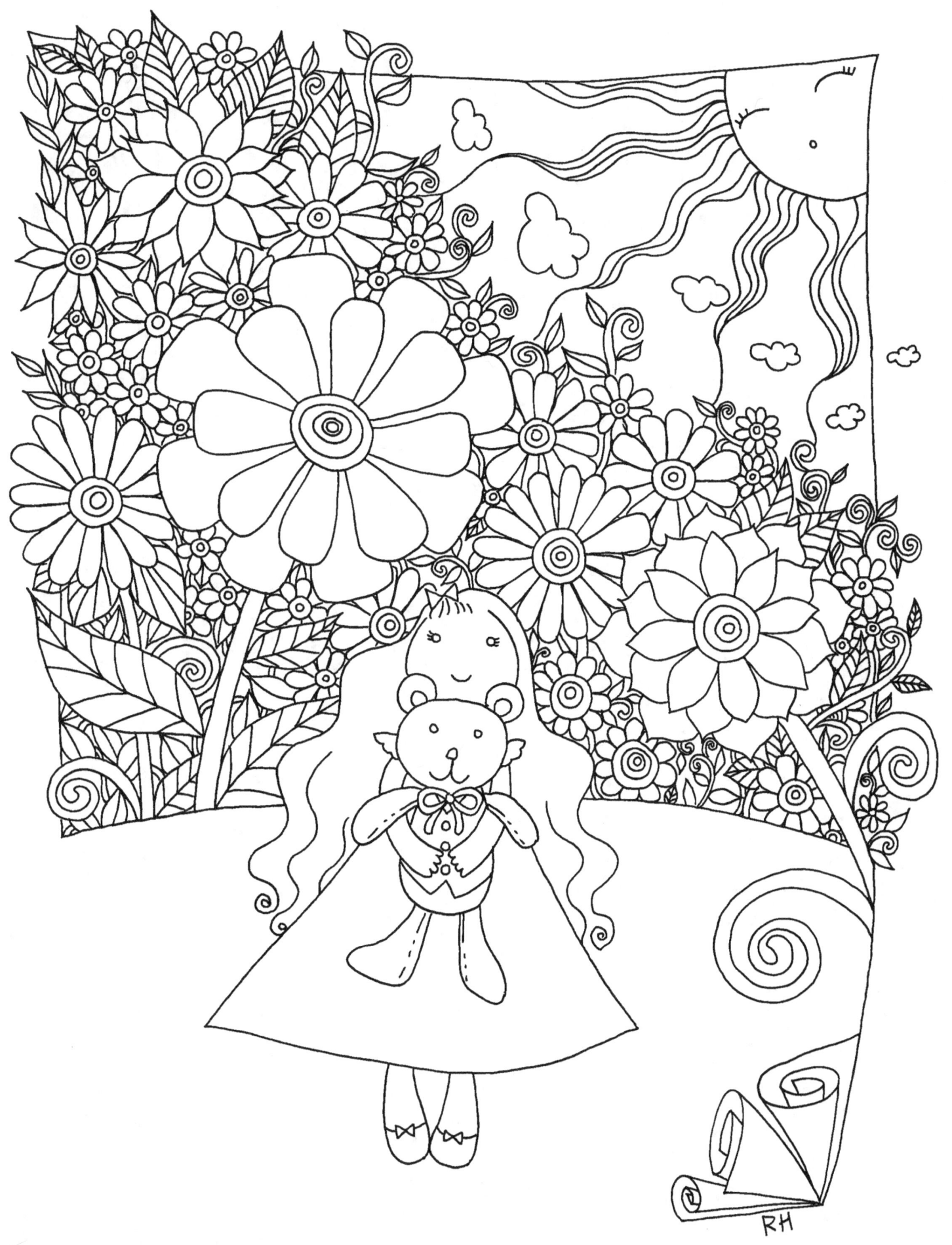

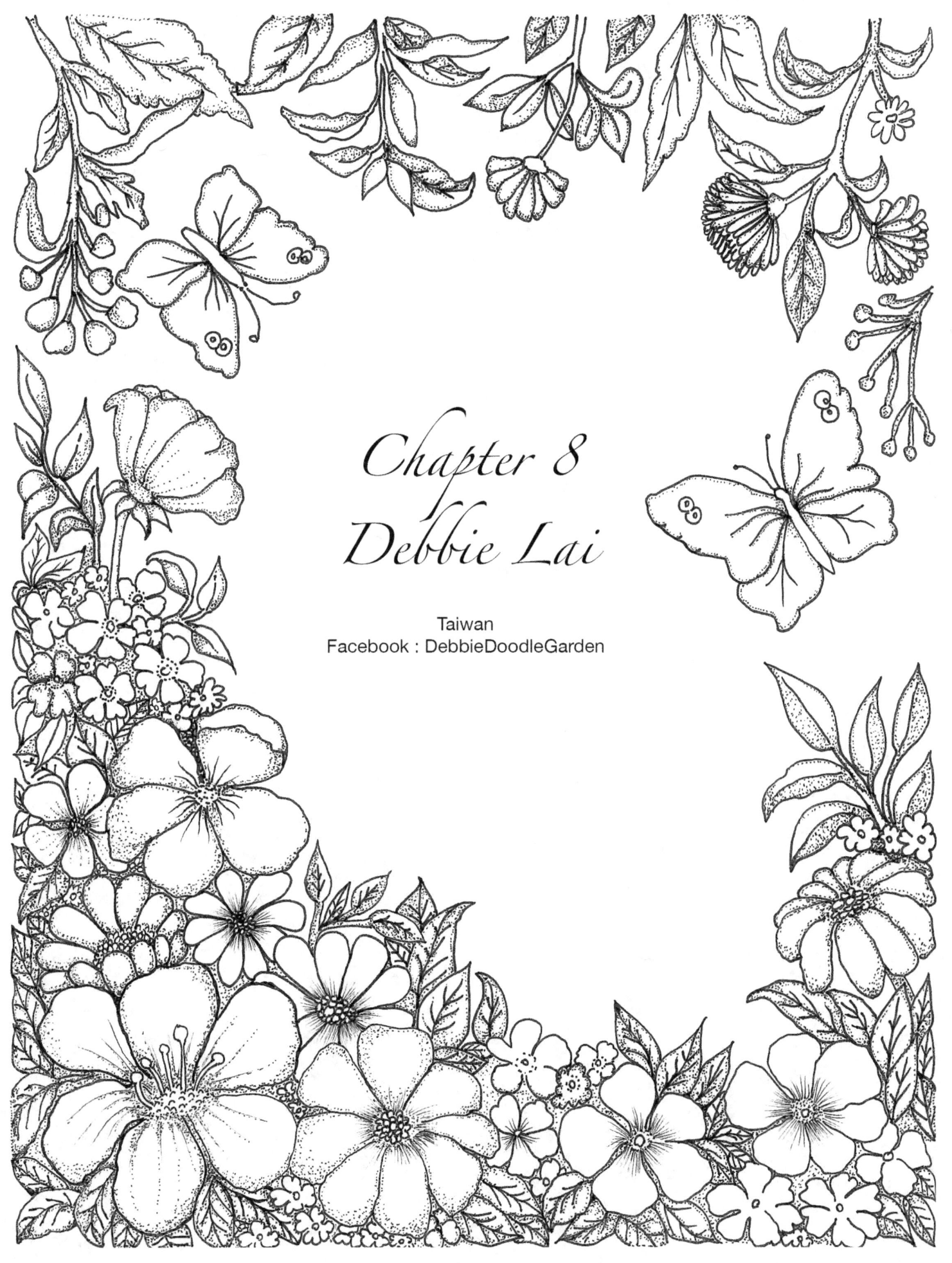

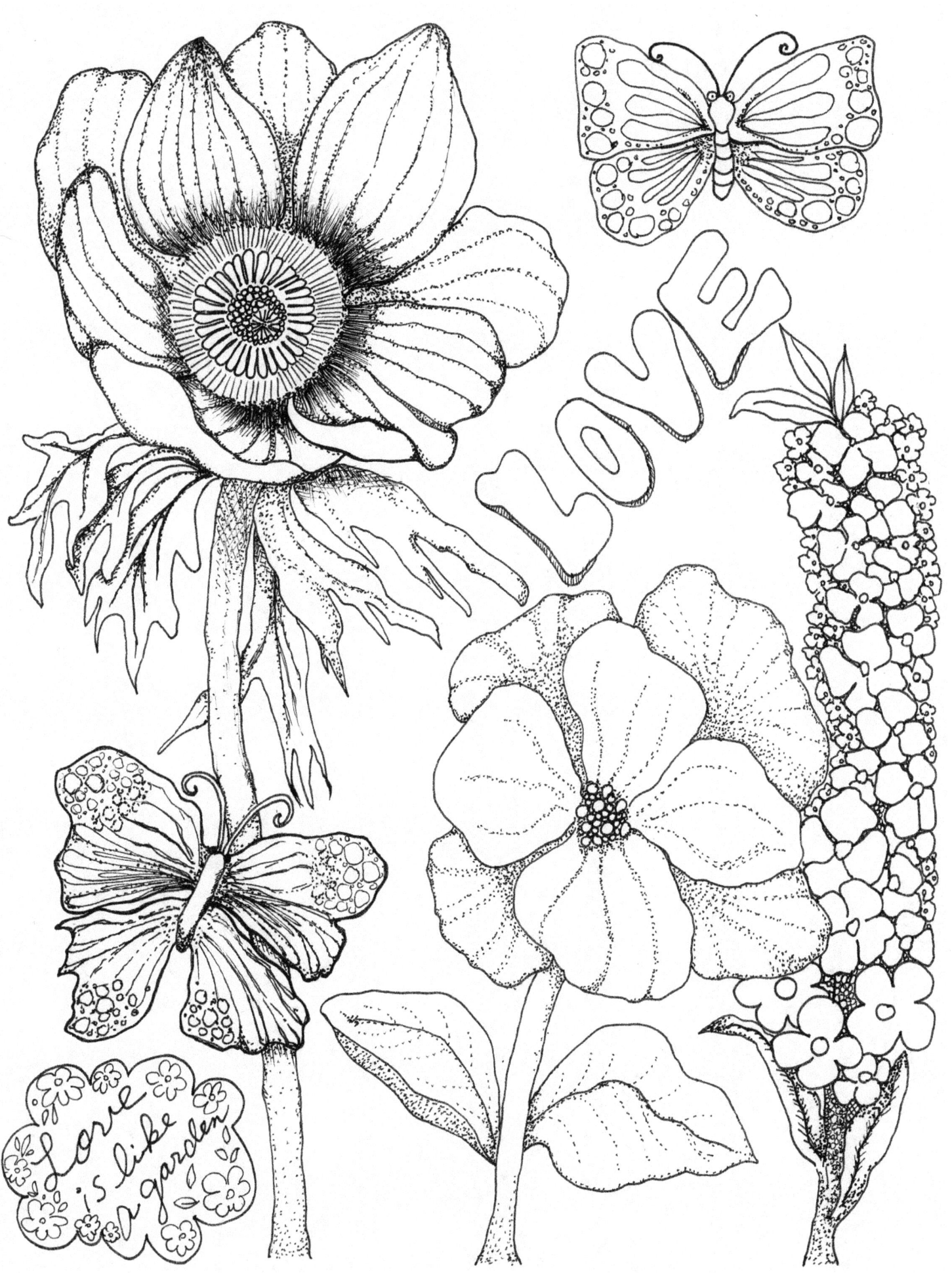

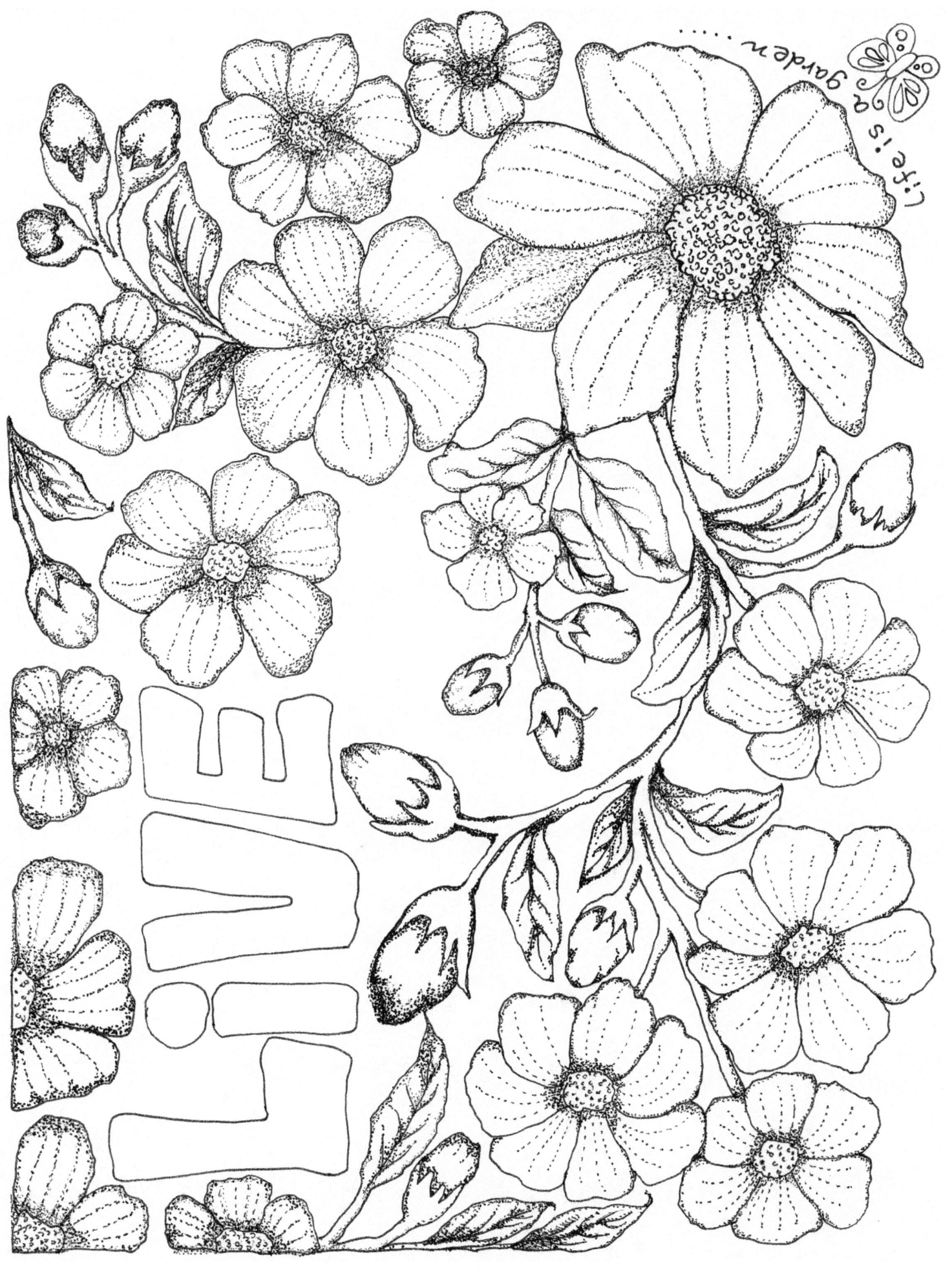

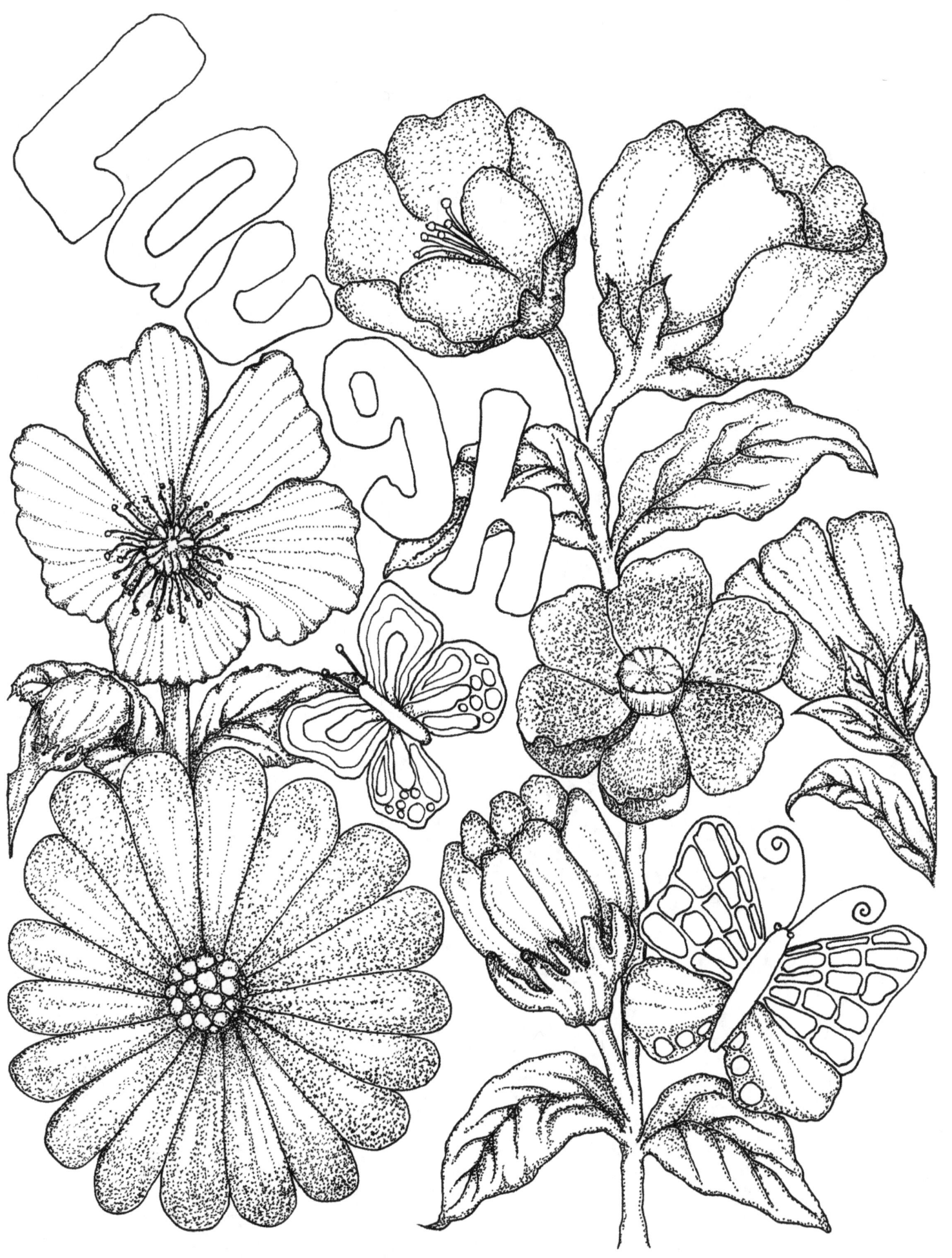

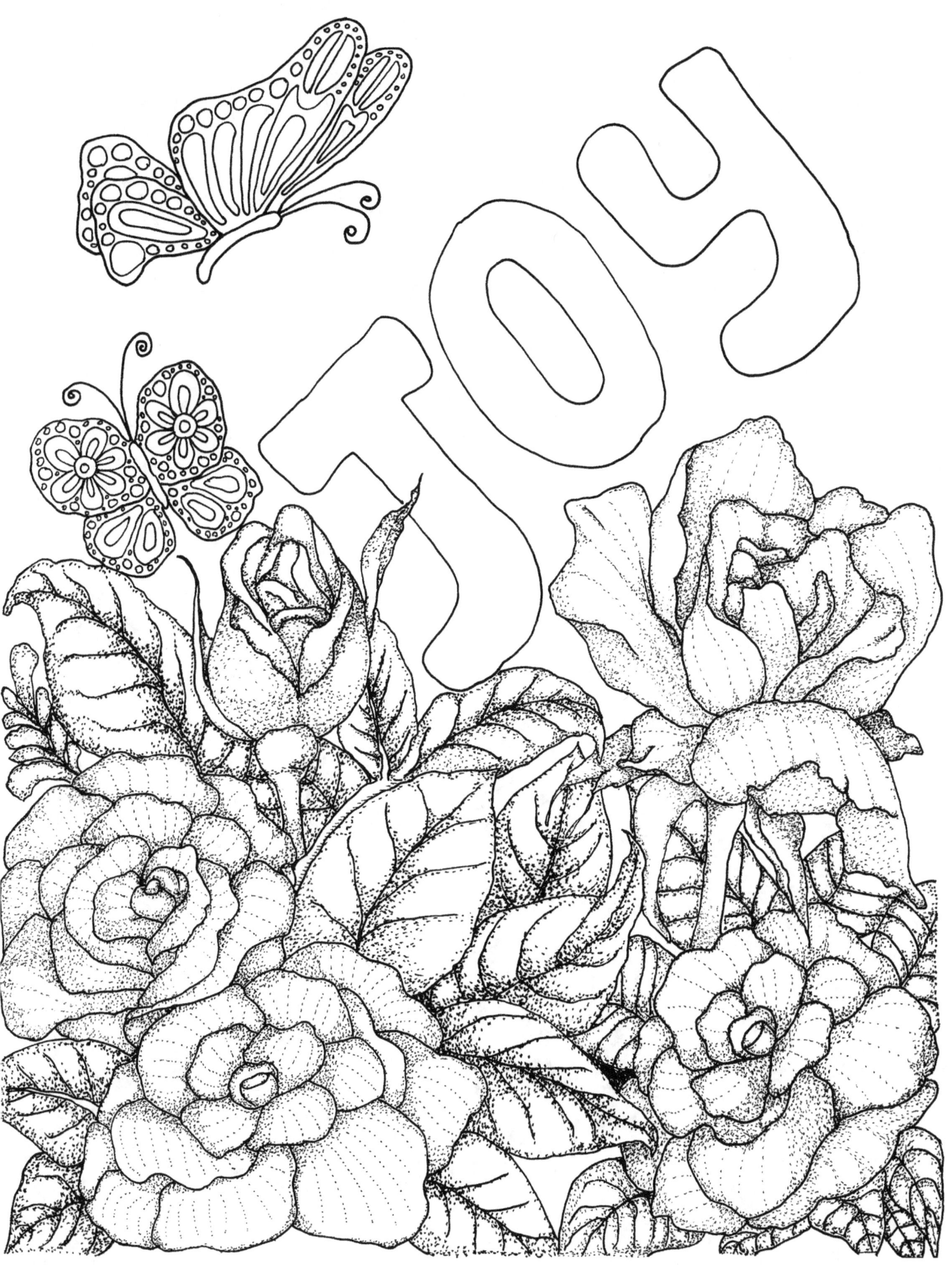

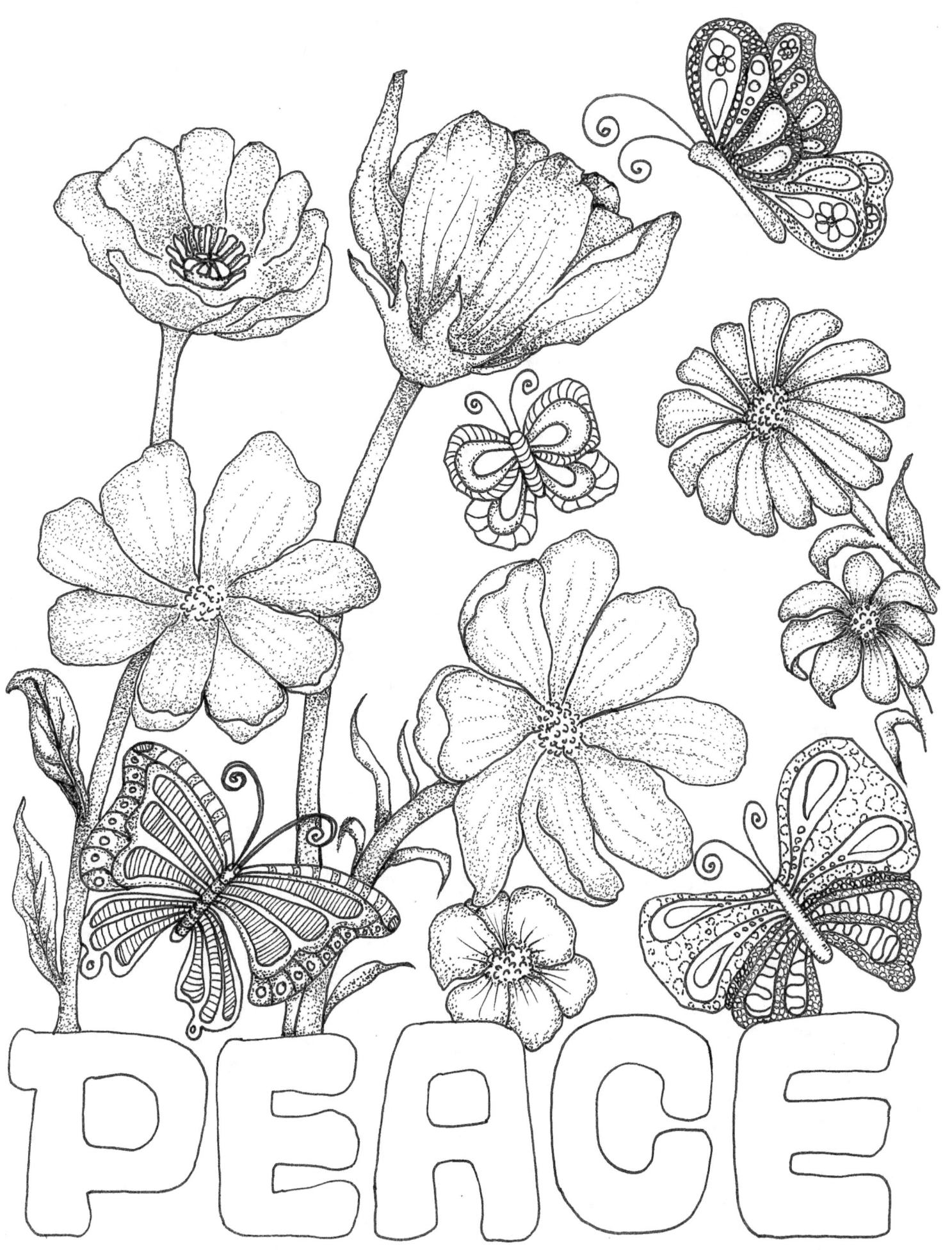

Chapter 9
Lilan Chen

Taiwan
Facebook : lilanchen.art

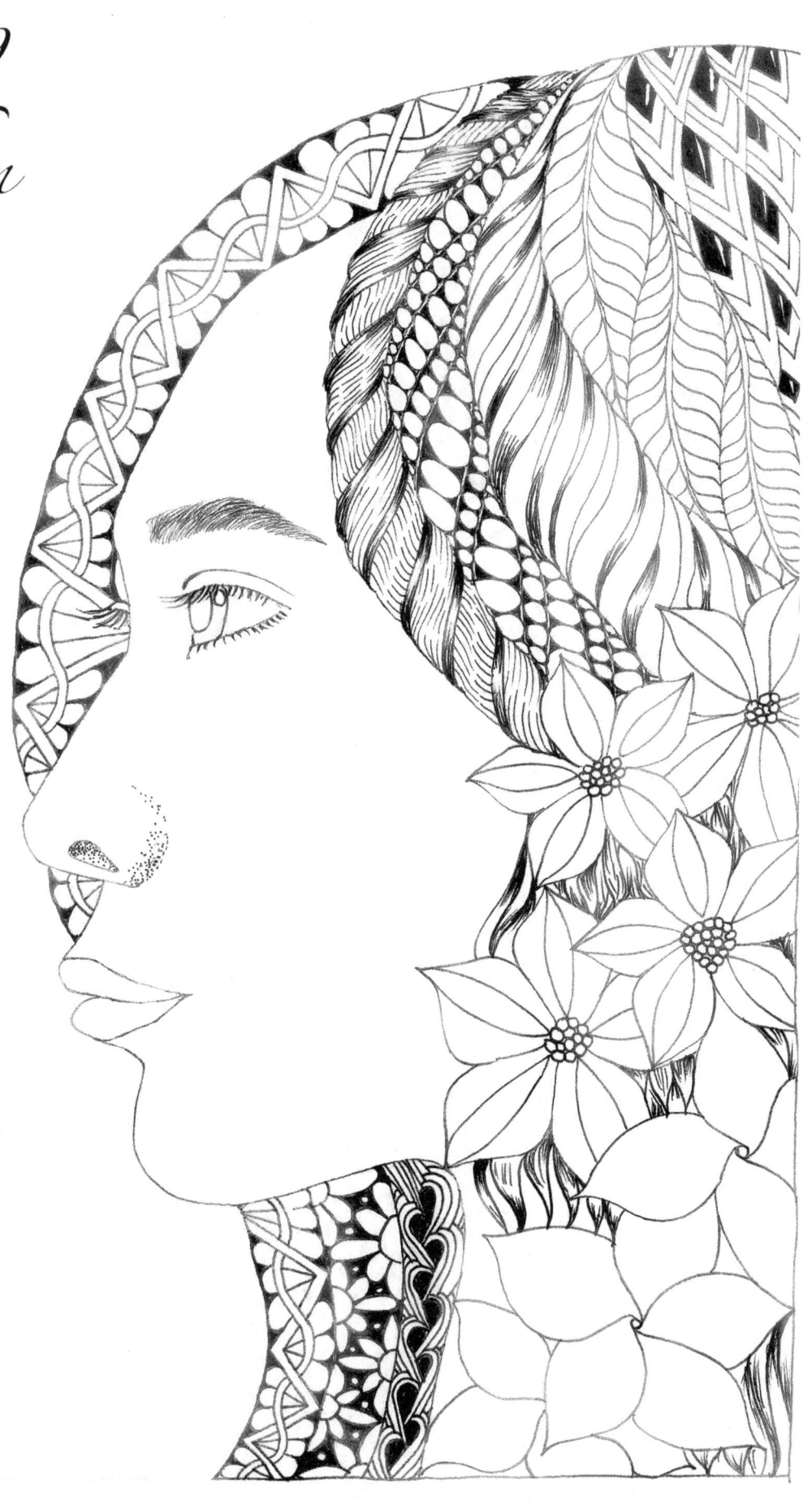

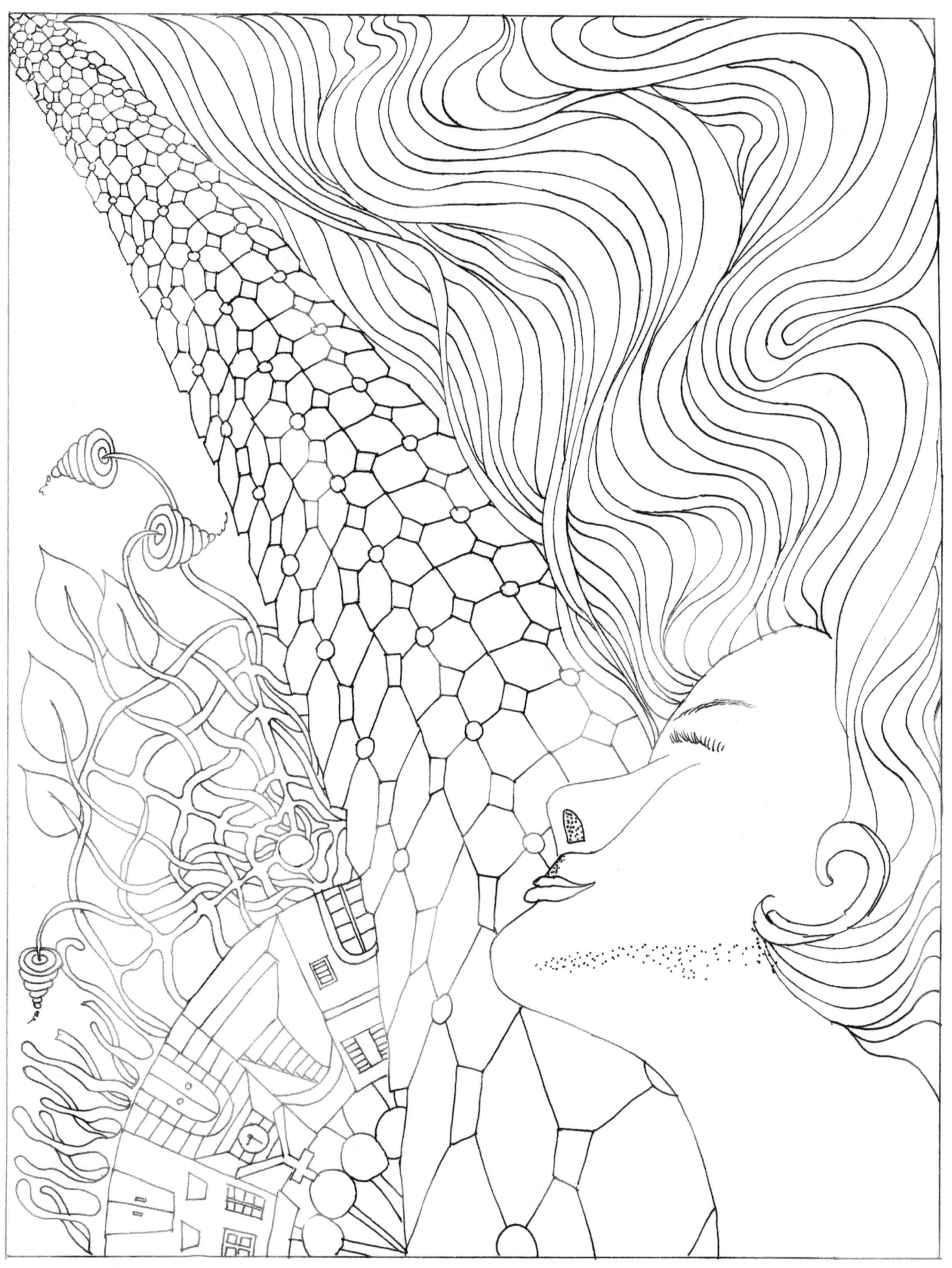

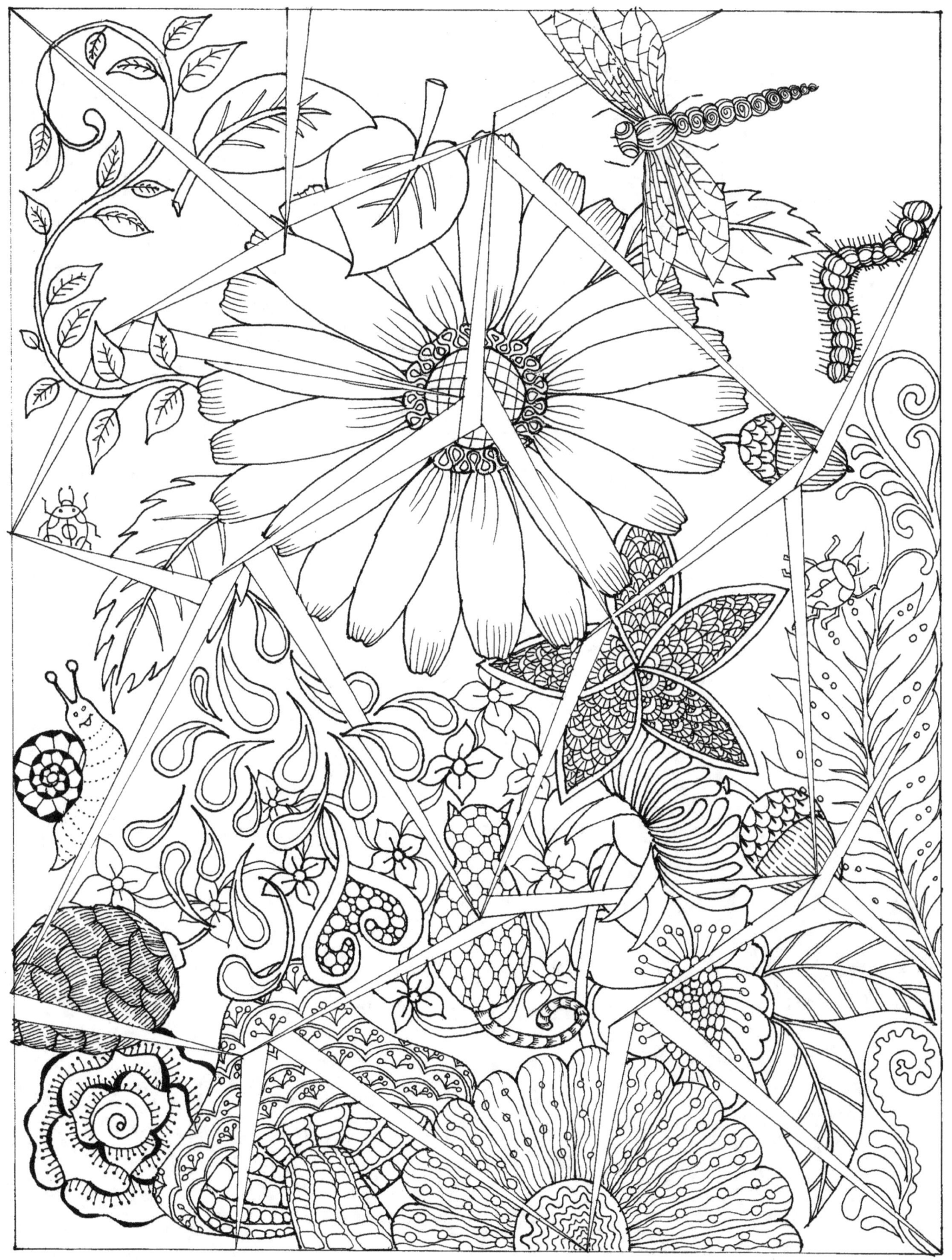

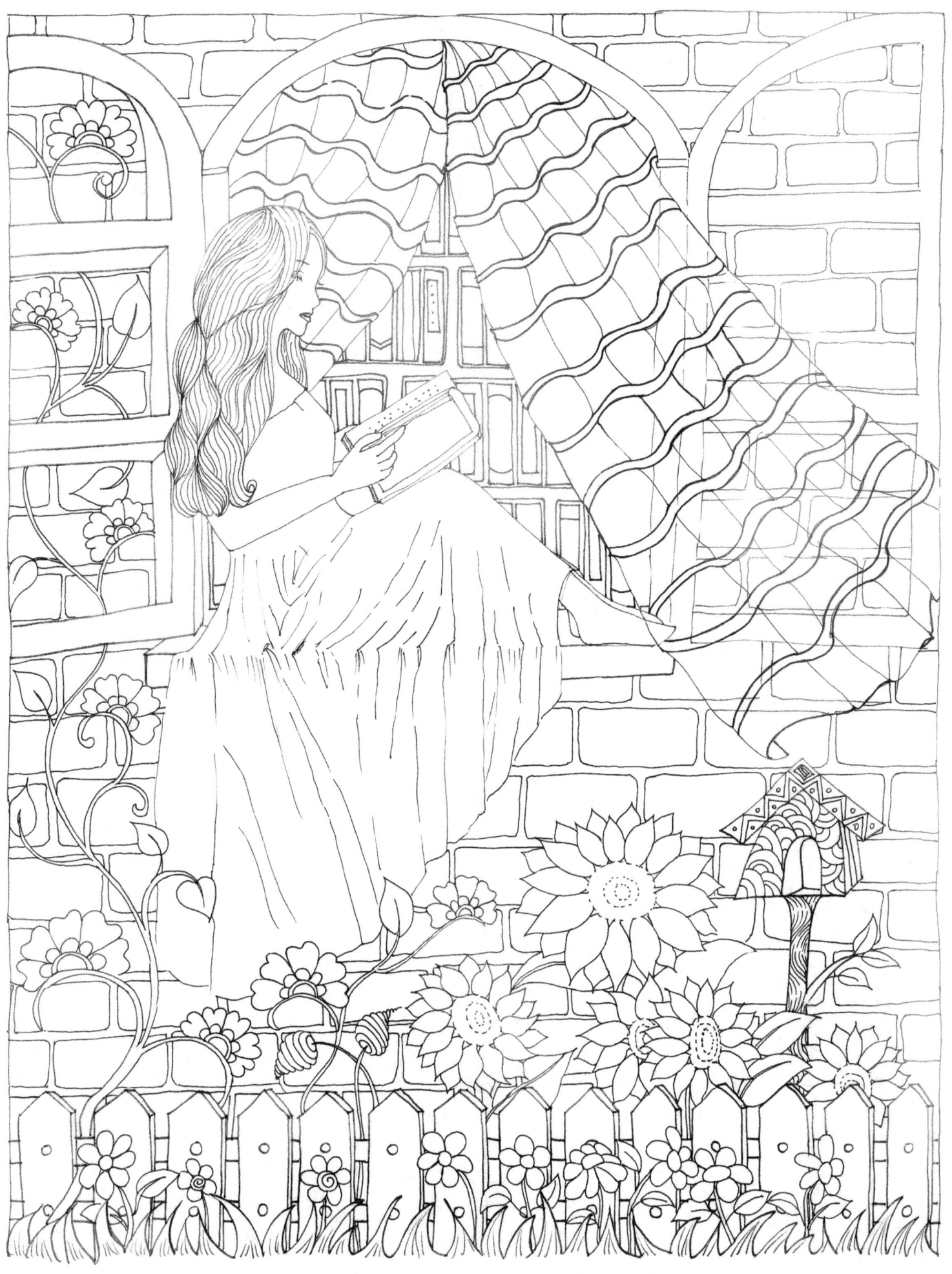

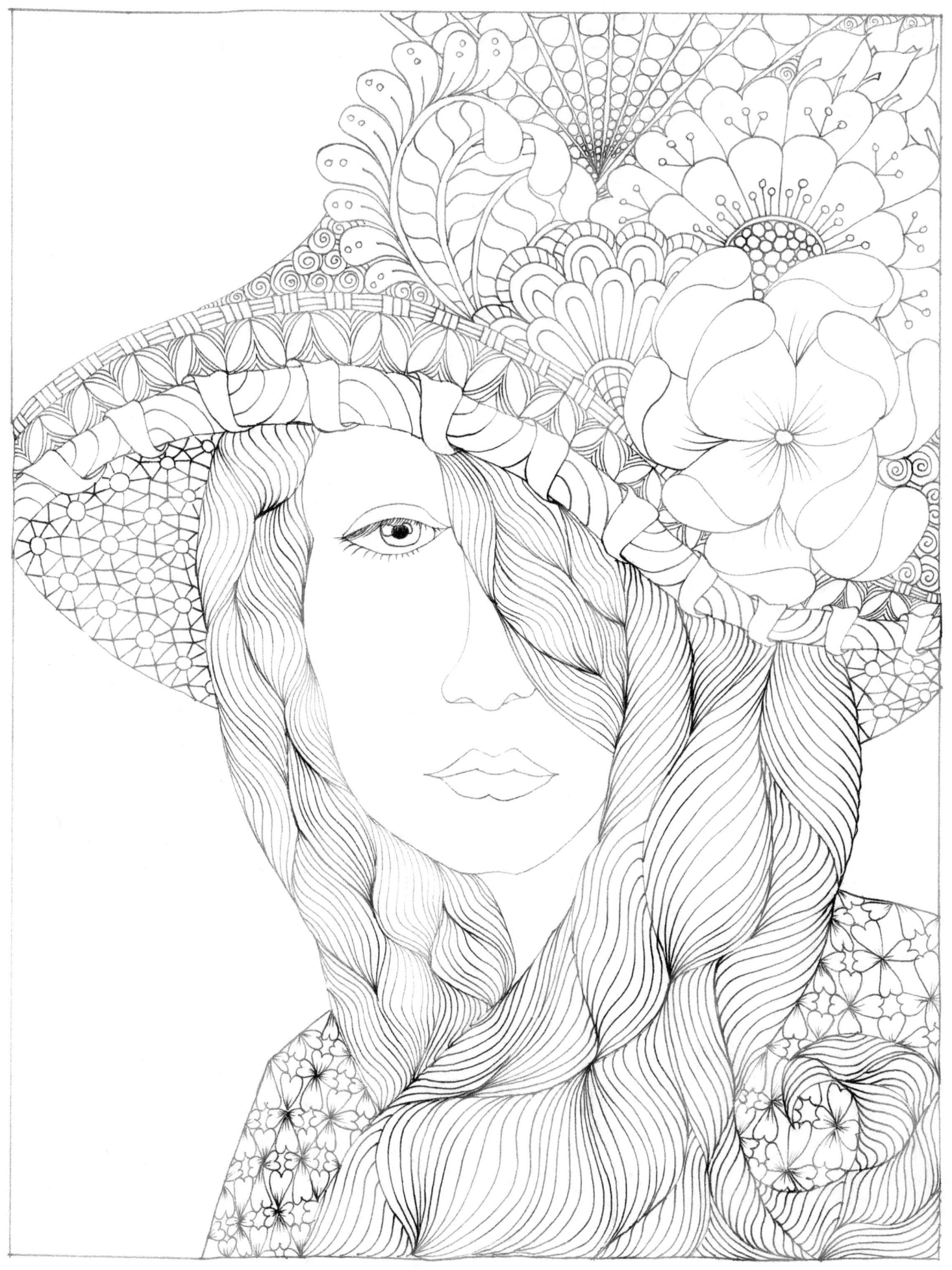

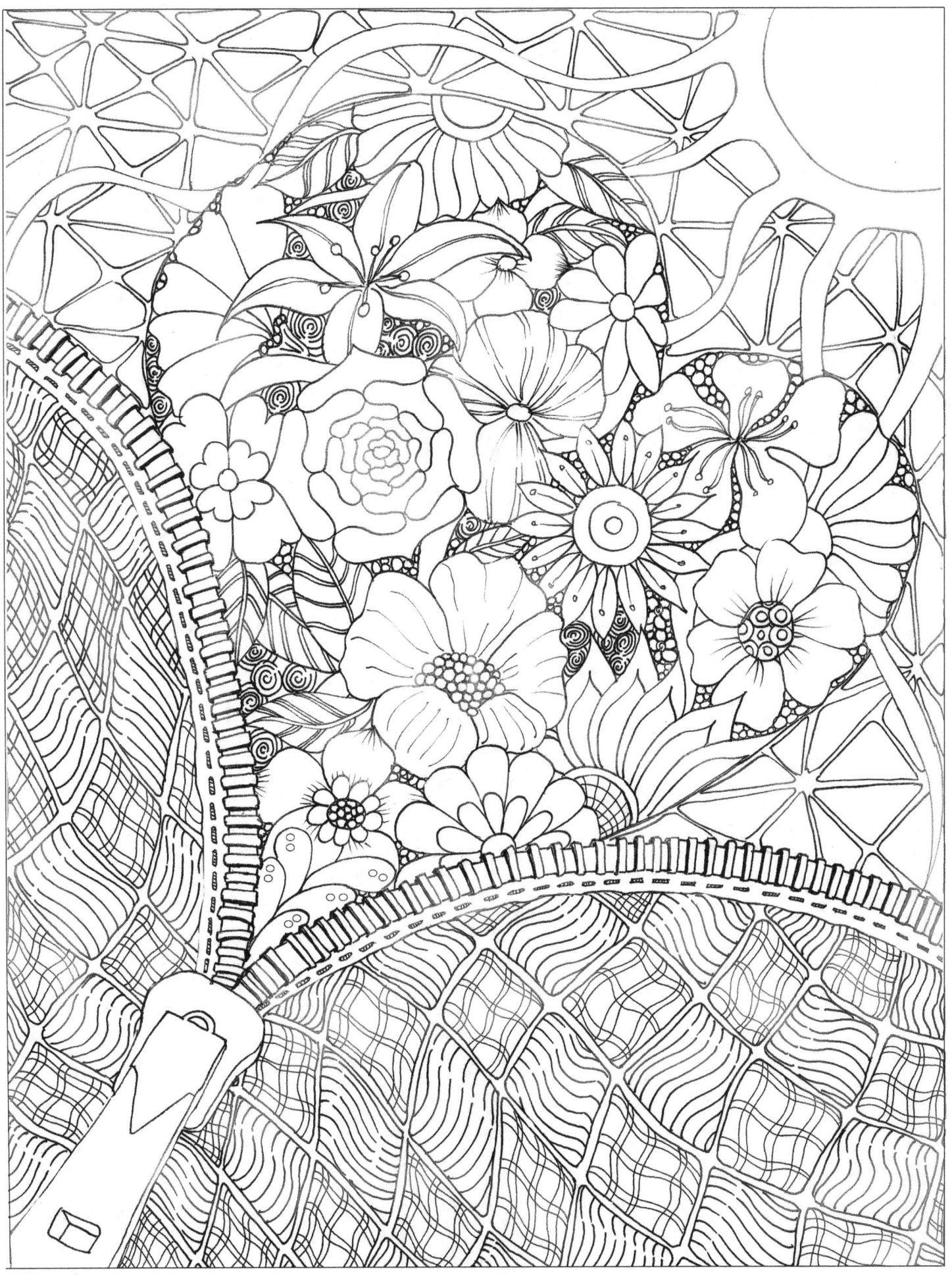

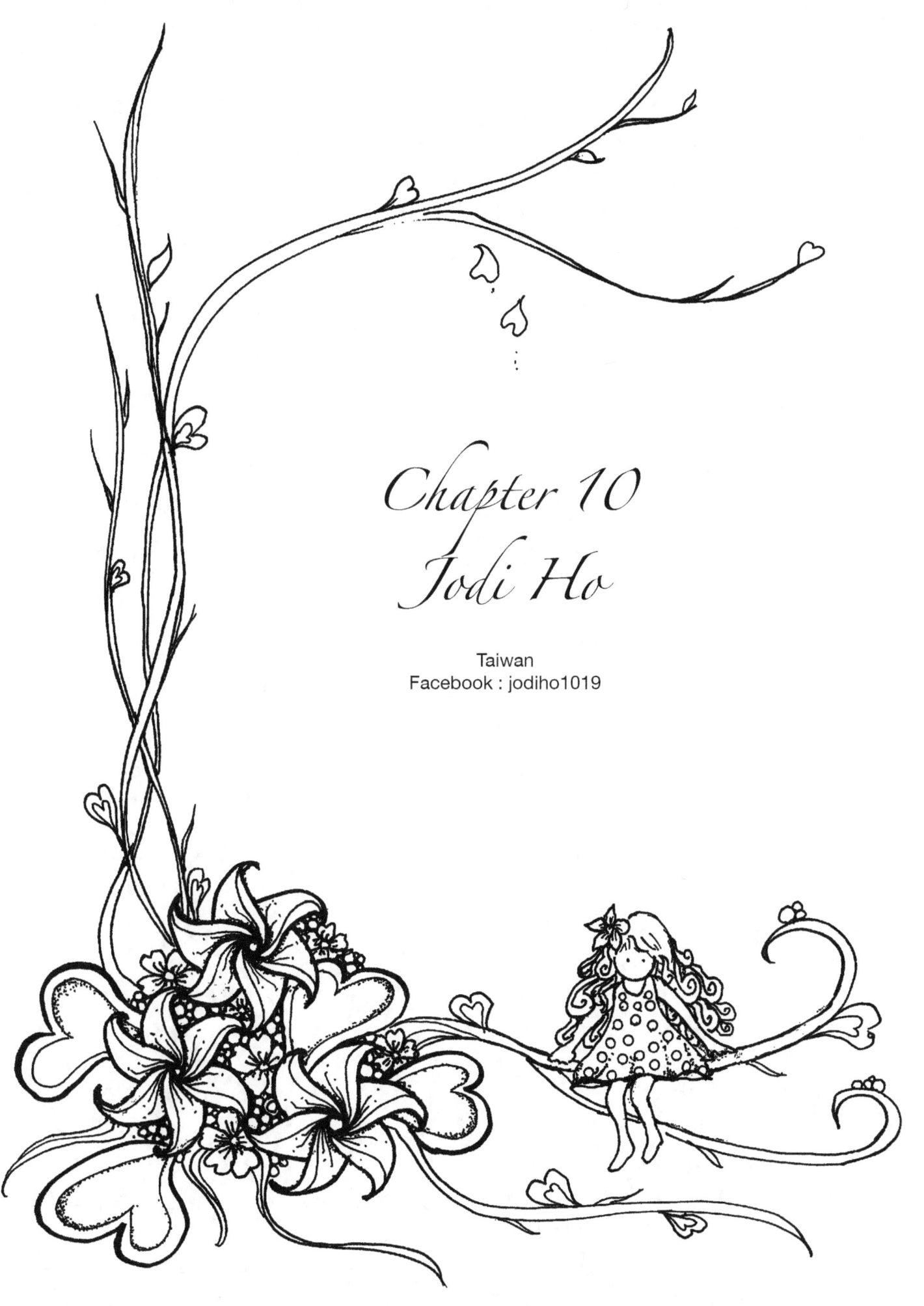

Chapter 10
Jodi Ho

Taiwan
Facebook : jodiho1019

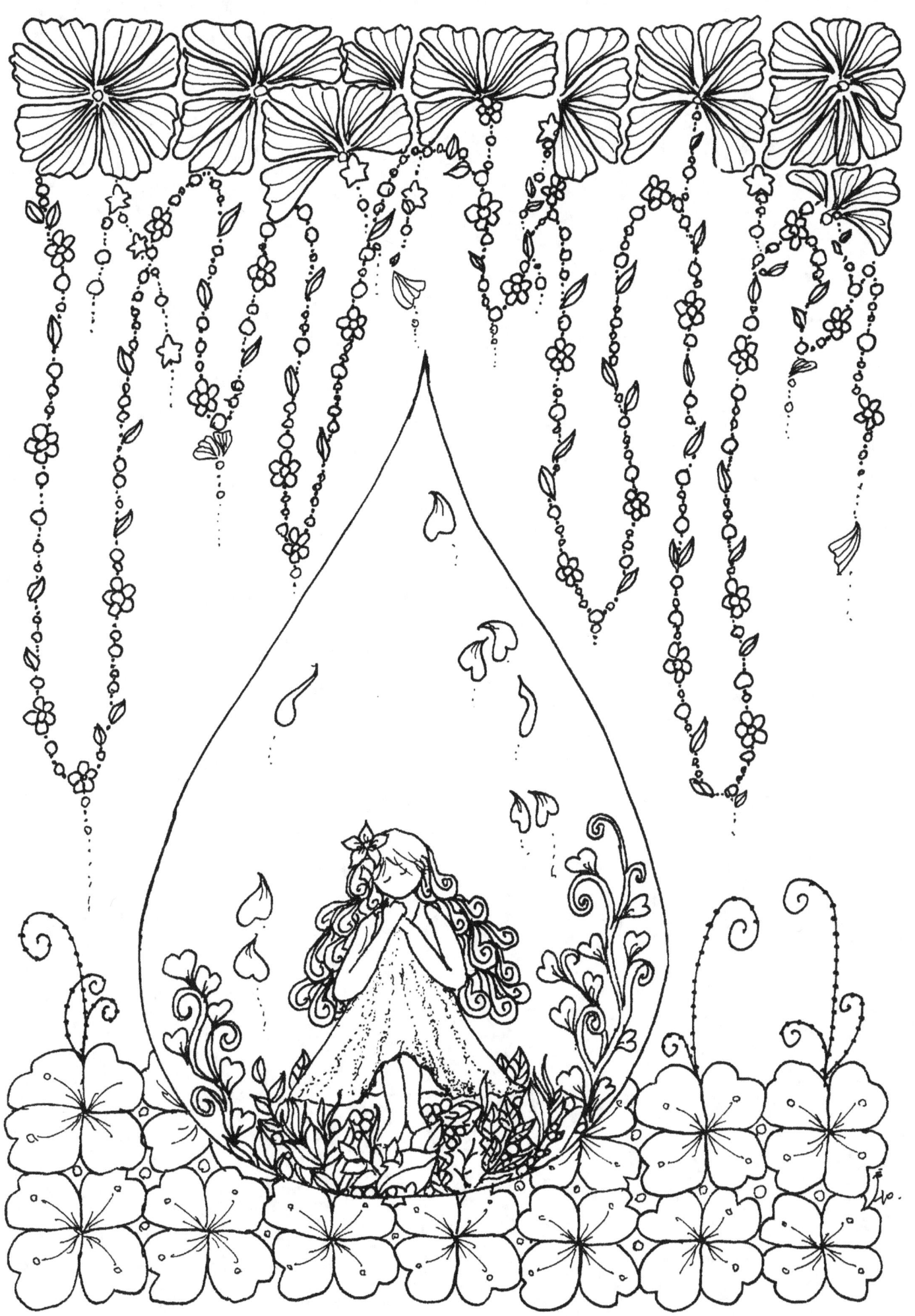

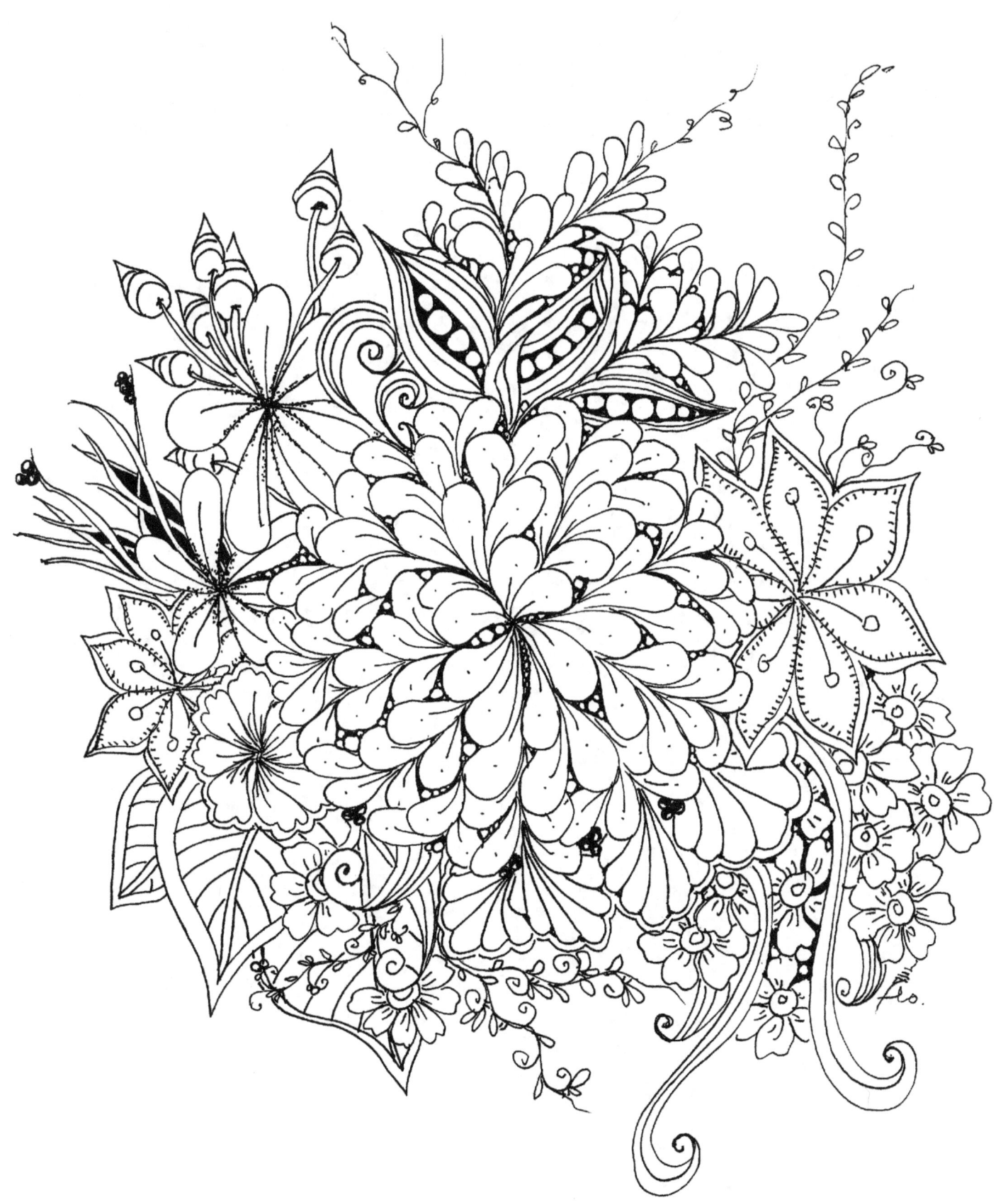

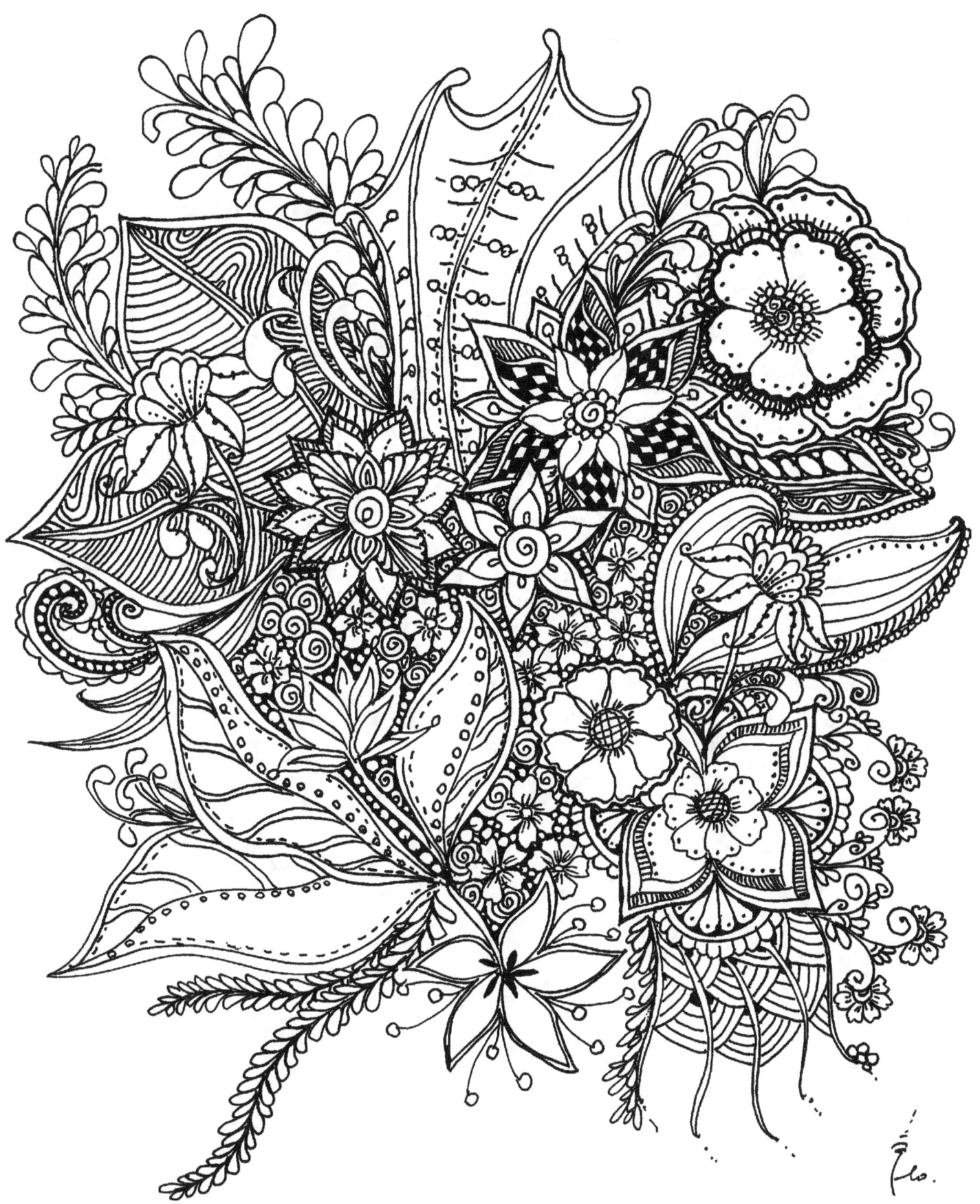

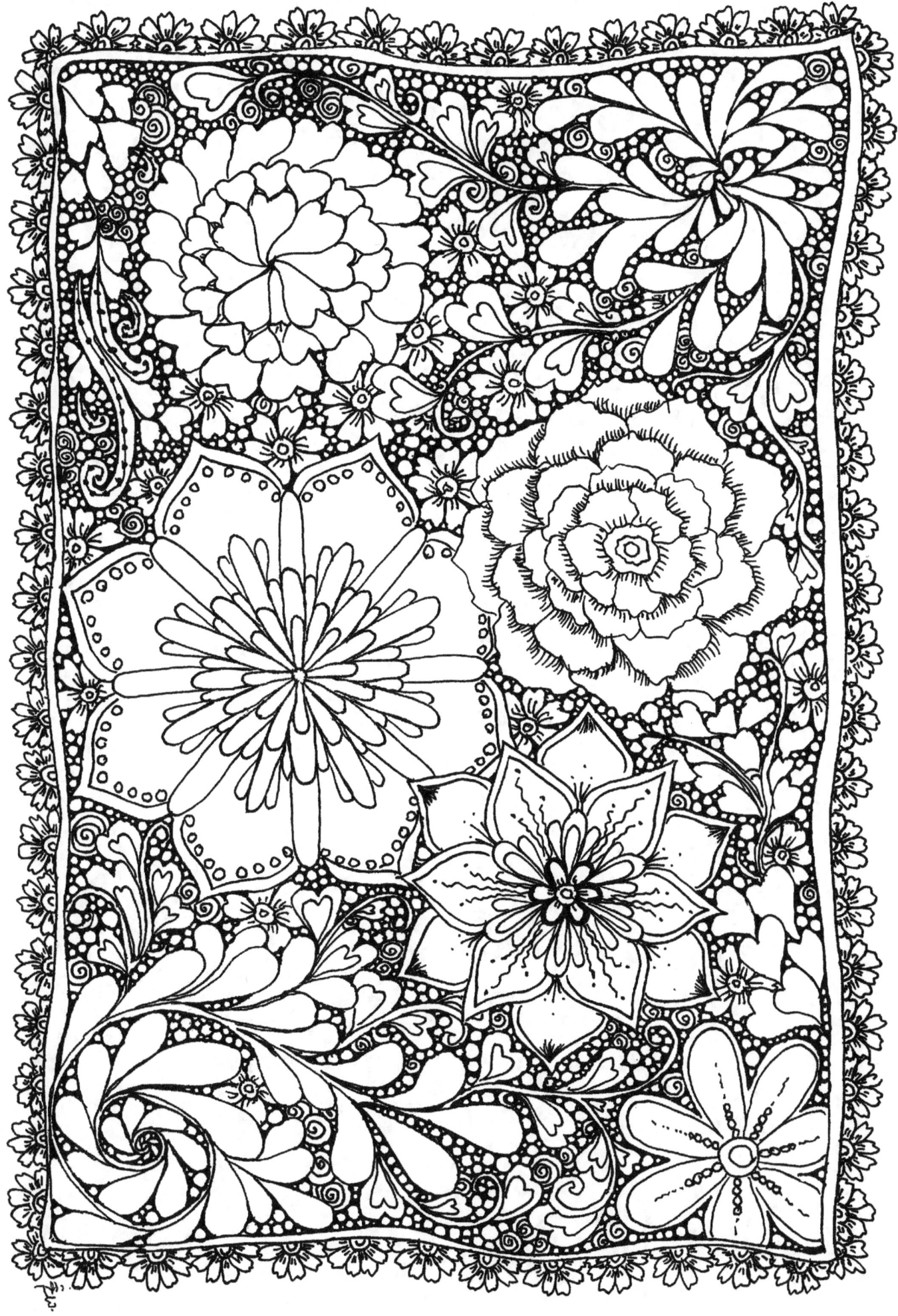

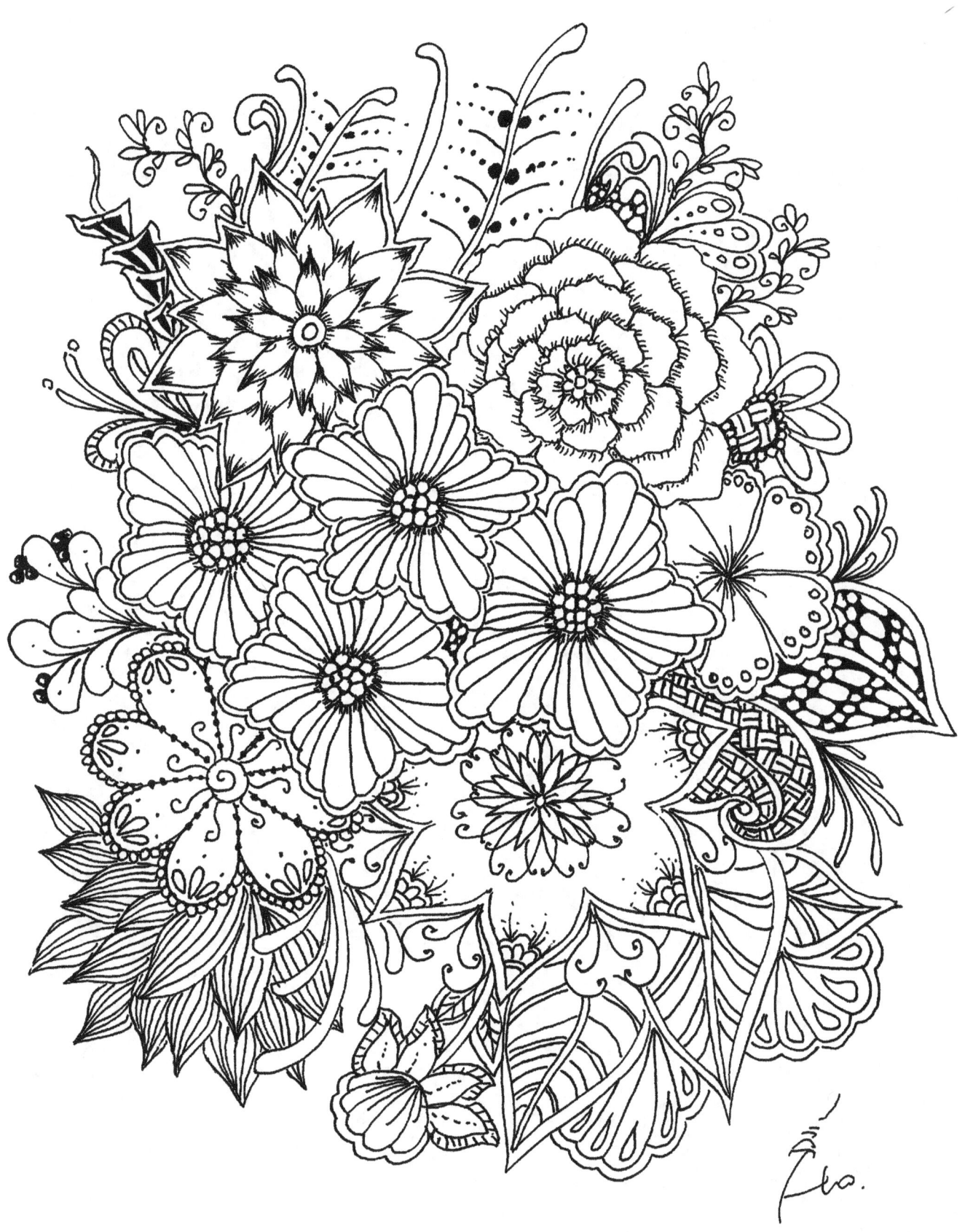

We from Global Doodle Gems, hope your journey through our book has been a pleasant one!

Please feel free to share your colored versions with us here:

https://www.facebook.com/groups/globaldoodlegems/

In our group you can meet the artists and enjoy exclusive freebies, video previews and participate in our community books "Colorists Choice" and so much more….

if you are wishing, that you could have the Chapter pages without the text, well then swing on by the group and get them for free in the freebie pdf for volume 12

Are you curious about Volume 13? ….well, just take a look at the next 2 pages and you will know what to exspect in the next volume of "Global Doodle Gems!

"Global Doodle Gems" Volume 13
Preview

Velvet Comeau

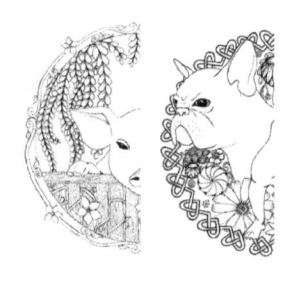 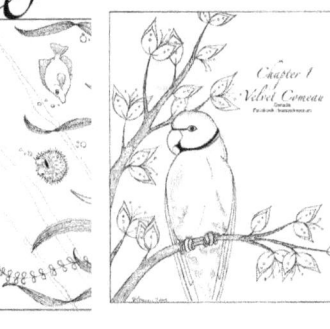 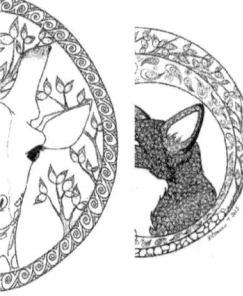

MWMS
Johanna Ans

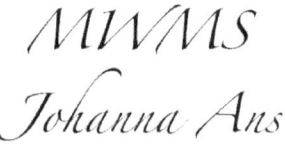 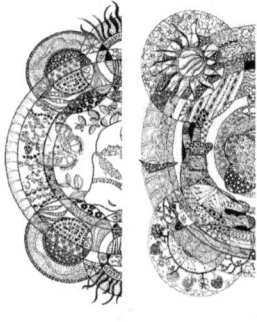 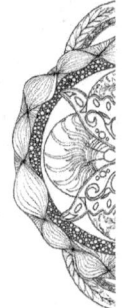 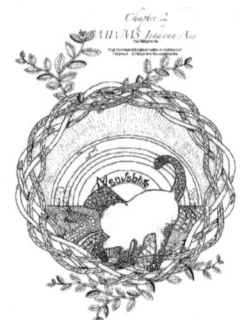 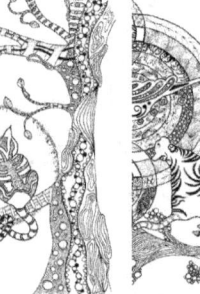

Wnyy Lin
Small Fish

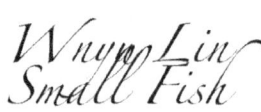 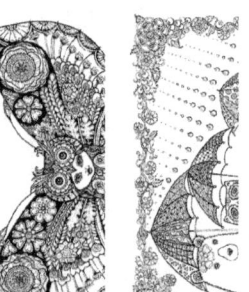 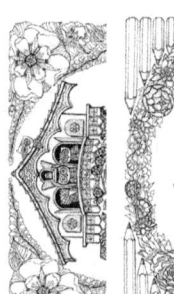 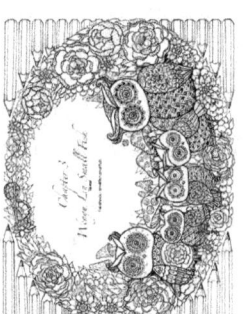 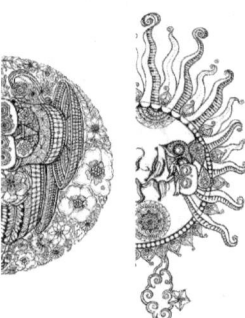

Peggy Sue's Art

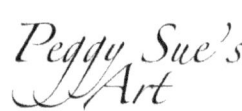 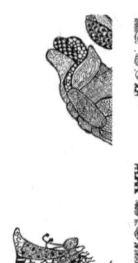 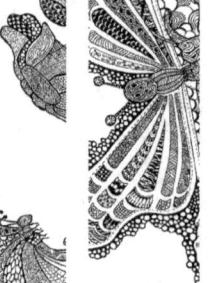 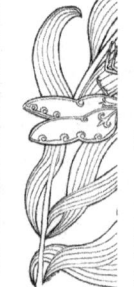 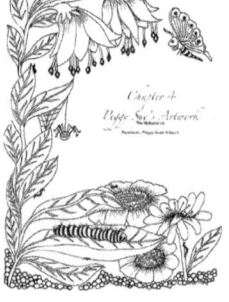 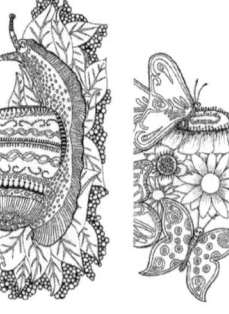

Yaya

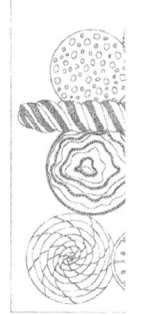 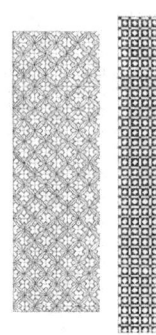 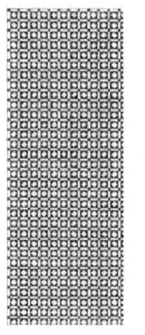 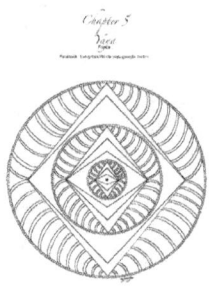 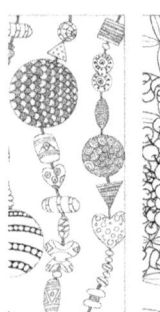 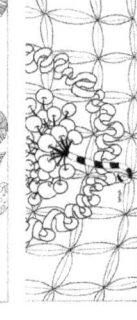

Creative Rosalien

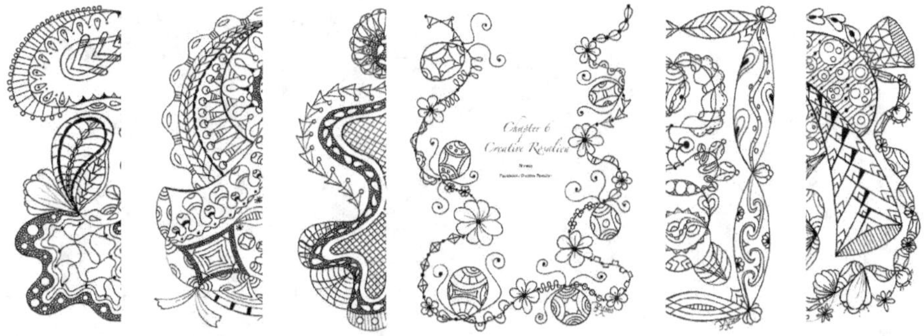

Adriana Garzia Volpe

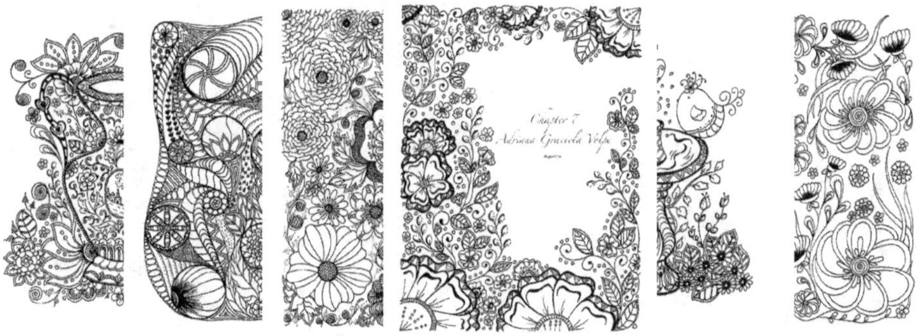

Angel Huang

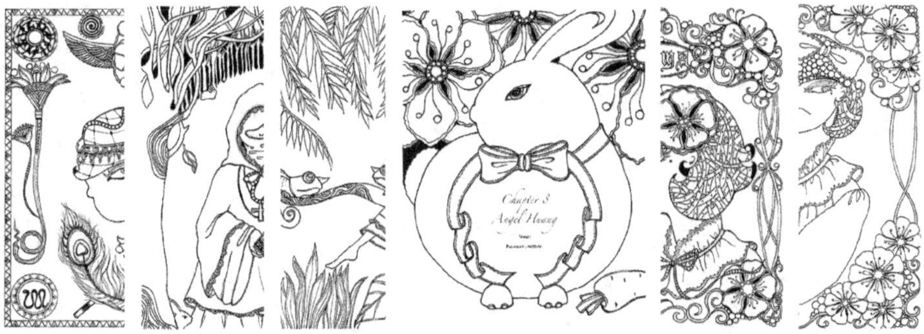

Audrey Sagh

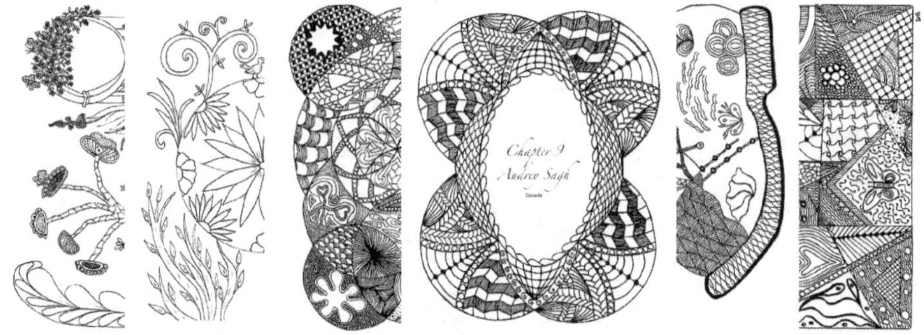

Ahmed Fouad Eid

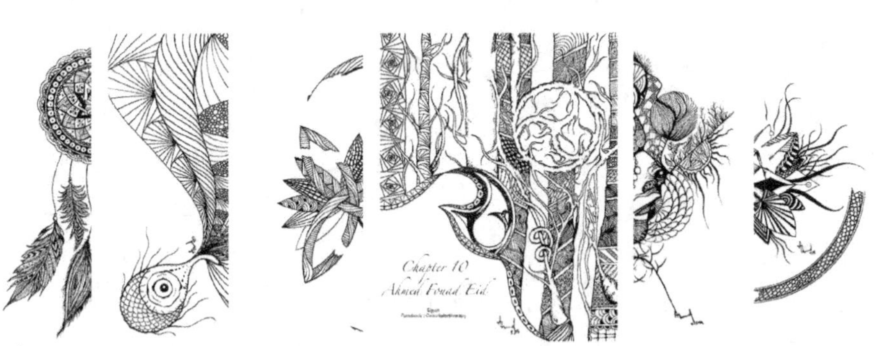

Meet the artists feautured in "GDG" Volume 13

Test Your Colors here ....
Charts from "My Pocket Color Companion"
and
"My Color Companion"

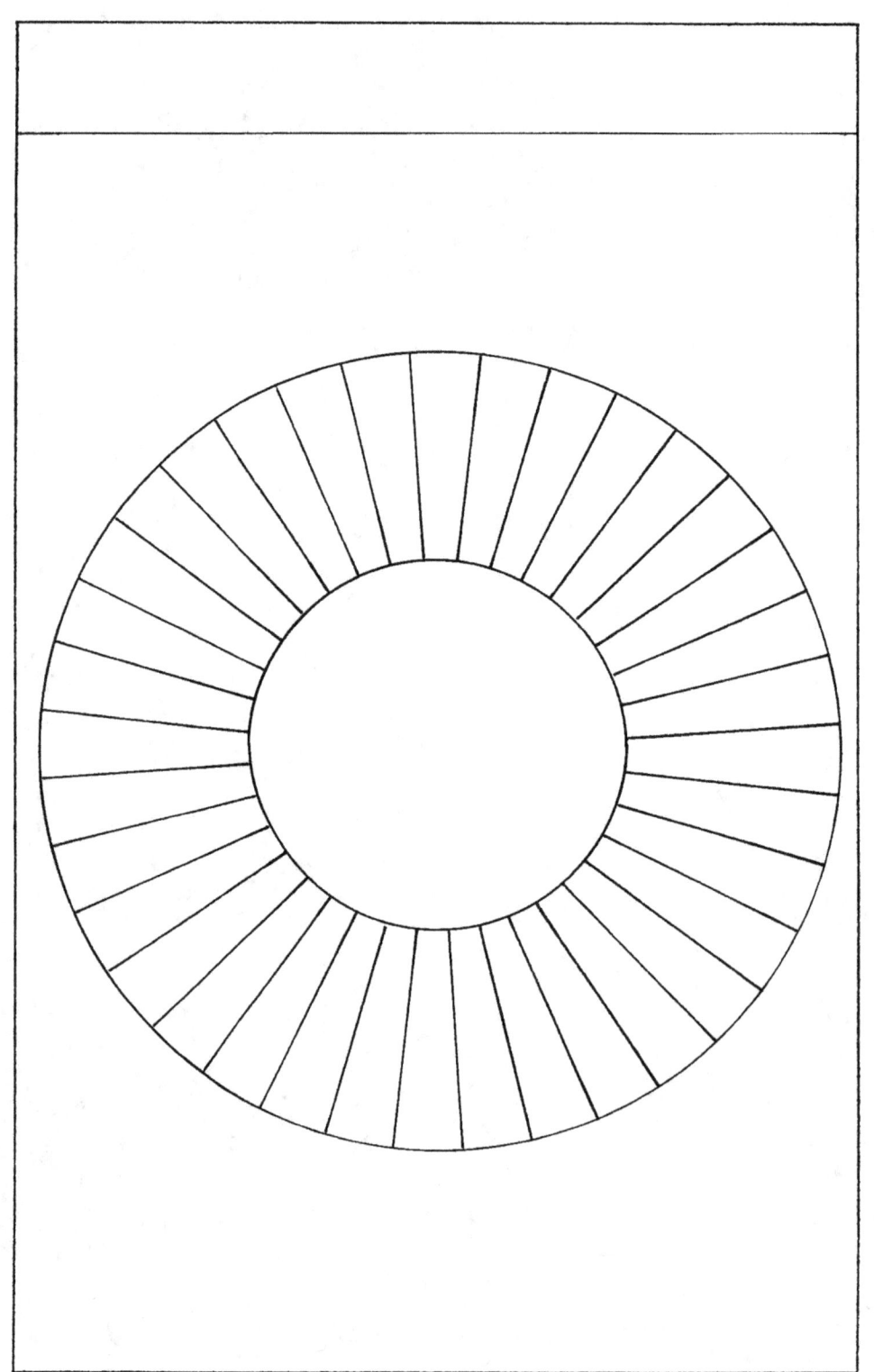

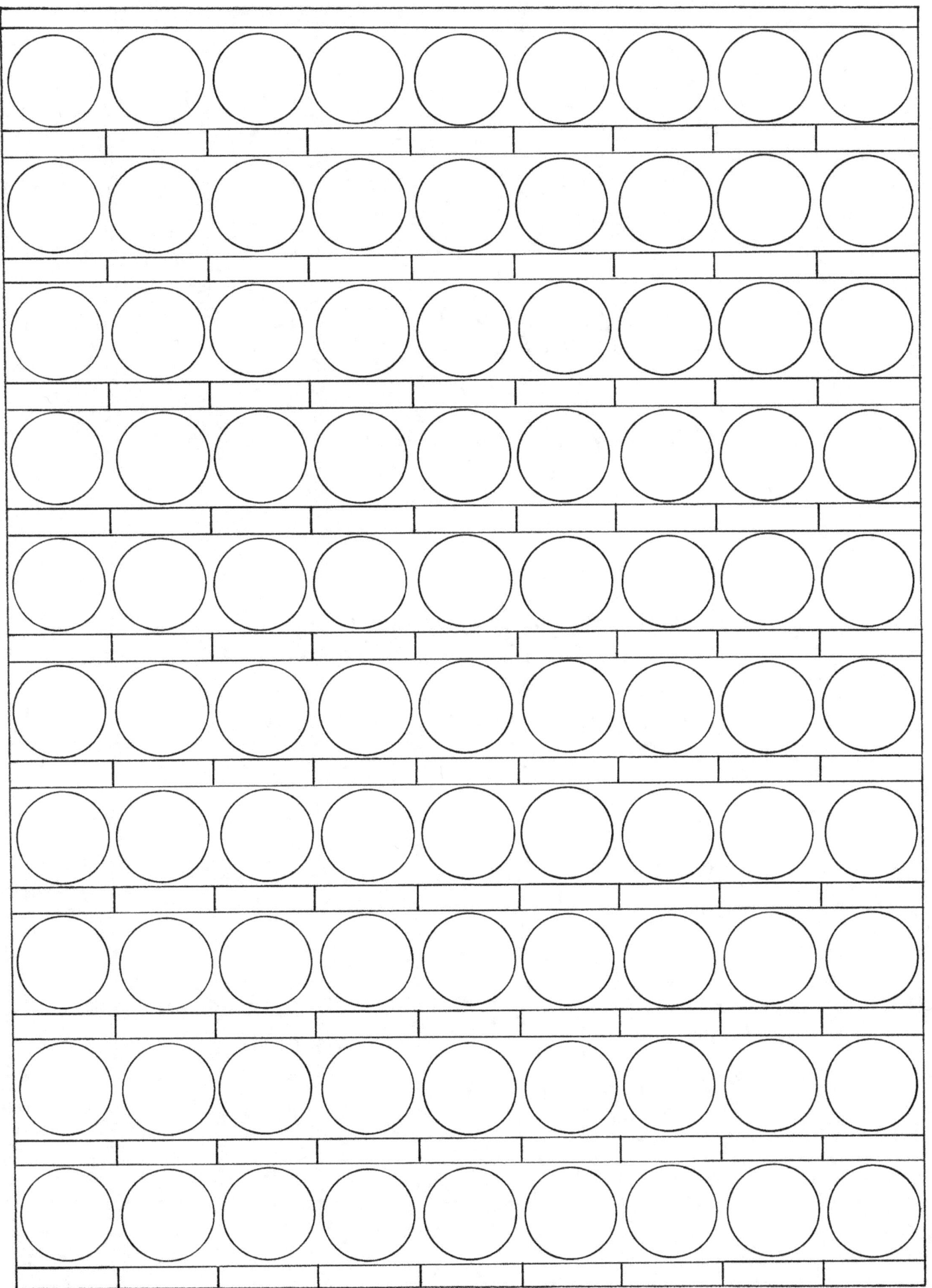

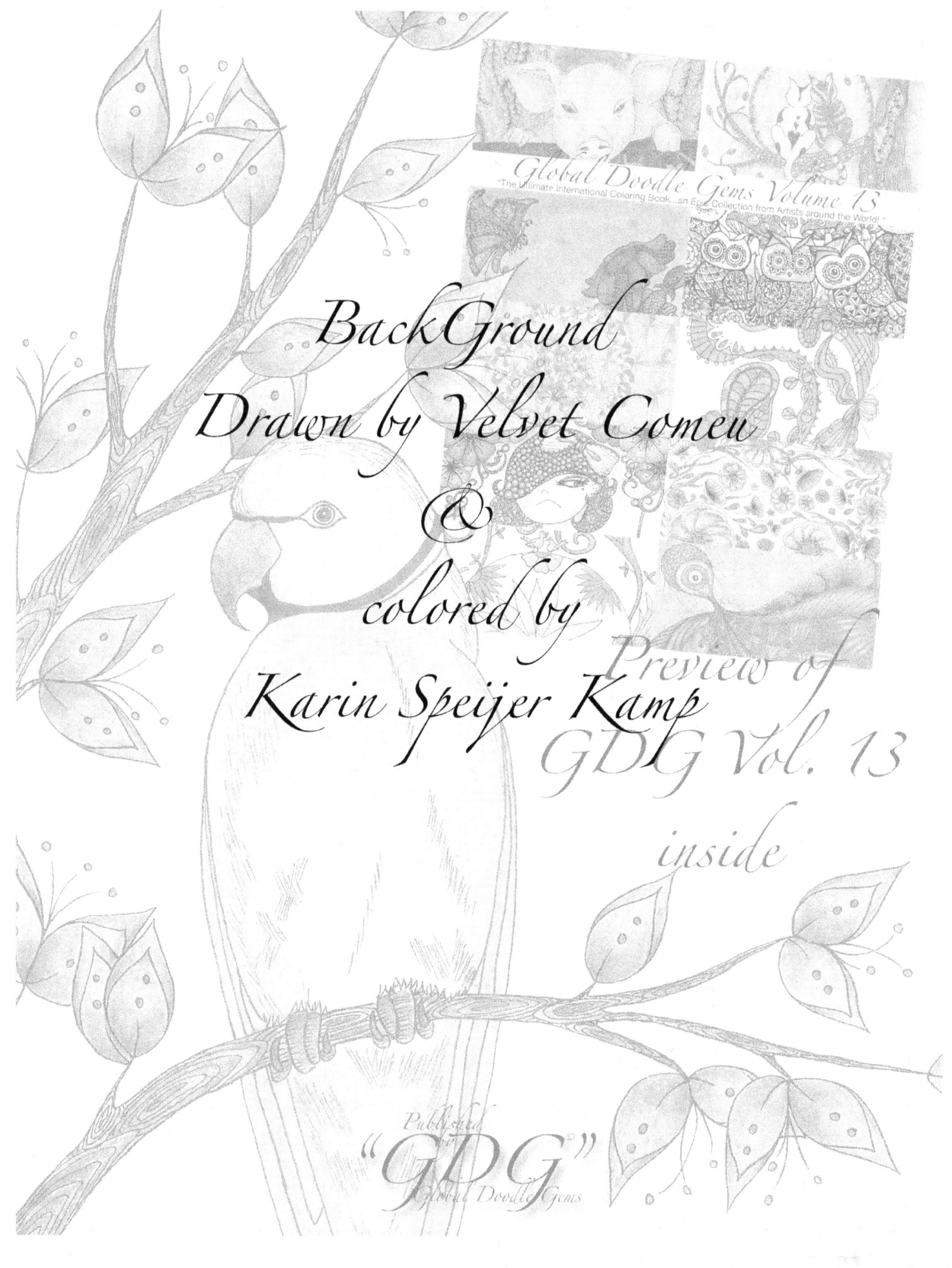

www.ingramcontent.com/pod-product-compliance
Lightning Source LLC
Chambersburg PA
CBHW082207220526
45470CB00010B/3074